THANKYOUOLOGY

How the Art of Saying Thank You
Transforms Your Life!

Cheryl Russell

Outskirts Press, Inc.
Denver, Colorado

THANKYOUOLOGY
How The Art of Saying Thank You Transforms Your Life!
All Rights Reserved.
Copyright © 2008 Cheryl Russell
V3.0 R1.1

Outskirts Press, Inc.
http://www.outskirtspress.com

ISBN: 978-1-4327-1924-1

Outskirts Press and the "OP" logo are trademarks belonging to Outskirts Press, Inc.

PRINTED IN THE UNITED STATES OF AMERICA

A Special *Thank You* Note

To "Little Cheryl" who wrote my first book, *The Story of the StarHearts*. *Thank you* for helping me write this one!

To my family, in particular my Mommy Dear, my sister, Susie, her husband, Steve, and their children—my nephew, Nicholas, and niece, Tara. *Thank you* for cheering me on with your unconditional light and love. I am forever grateful.

To my family of friends, I share this thought with you from Nancy Spain: "There are people whom one appreciates immediately and forever. Even to know they are alive in the world is quite enough." *Thank you* for being a wonderful part of my world.

To my family of mentors at large who have shared your gratitude wisdom from the podium and on the printed page. Learning from your truths encouraged me to share mine. *Thank you.*

And, to my Universe:

I acknowledge the principles of gratitude
saying thank you in unlimited ways,
I am grateful for everything I receive
to you, Spirit, I give all the praise.

Contents

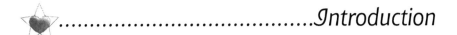 ....*Introduction*

The StarHeart Angel Brigade
has an important message for you,
Read each word carefully
to know what to do.

THANKYOUOLOGY is my story of how, when, where and why to say *thank you* with your thoughts, words and actions. As a *thank you* coach, I believe the power of *thank you* ignites your spirit to transform your health, relationships, success on the job and more. When you live the art of saying *thank you* each day, you create a most magnificent way of life. And, here is how:

Having health challenges? Feeling mentally or emotionally exhausted? THANKYOUOLOGY is for your mind, body and spirit. Chapter five is filled to the brim with ideas from head to toe and from A to Z. The more you say *thank you* to your body, the more it responds with dynamic health and well-being for you.

Struggling at home with a child, spouse or roommate? THANKYOUOLOGY is your key to rich and rewarding relationships. Chapter six offers a collection of *thank you* ideas that is sure to change how you acknowledge others and how they express their appreciation to you. And yes, *thank you* notes are more important than ever in today's world.

Finding it difficult to manifest your dreams or challenging to keep a positive outlook on life? THANK-YOUOLOGY is how you say *thank you* for everything before it happens, while it is happening and after it happens. Chapter seven gives you the confidence to say *thank you* with faith featuring an amazing once-in-a-lifetime story as encouragement. No fair peeking at chapter ten for an extra little twist! And, if rules or a list of steps are too much for you to remember, chapter nine has the answer: There are no rules!

What is it that prompted me to write THANKYOU-OLOGY? Everyone has a story and mine is profoundly shaped by two simple words, *thank you*.

Traveling solo around the world in 1980-81, I found it was with a big smile and a sincere *thank you* that enabled me to achieve this life-changing journey. Upon my return, I frequently shared my philosophical perspectives as a guest on the Los Angeles television show, *There is a Way*, hosted by Unity minister, Dale Batesole. Those appearances launched my career as a motivational speaker and gave me the opportunity to teach many ideas for personal and professional growth.

Recognizing one of my passions is the joy of acknowledging others, I put that talent to work for nearly 15 years as a non-profit development director. In addition to raising the money, I LOVED saying *thank you* for it with award-winning events, tribute dinners and one-of-a-kind gifts of appreciation.

Reflecting on my beliefs and those of esteemed writers and speakers, it became obvious saying *thank you* was the key to transforming my life. *Thank you* is my mantra, my prayer, my heart and soul. That is why I had to write THANKYOUOLOGY—to put in writing, and share with you, the powerful *thank you* principles I love to live.

THANKYOUOLOGY is a natural segue from my first book, *The Story of the StarHearts*. Written in poetic verse for children of all ages, it is a story of how the StarHeart symbolizes light and love—a power I believe is actualized with a *thank you* consciousness. The more we think *thank you*, say *thank you* and feel *thank you*, the more we benefit from its unlimited energy.

After *The Story of the StarHearts* was published in 2001, I started writing a daily poem to give thanks and to affirm my intentions for the day. Poetic verse helps me quickly access what is on my mind and in my heart. As a result, I turn most anything into a poem—including a resignation letter from a job!

When THANKYOUOLOGY was bubbling in my head, it was no surprise that it began with a StarHeart story. I call it the *Reader's Digest* version and was delighted how each verse of the poem worked well as a chapter introduction. For a preview of the THANKYOUOLOGY philosophy, here is the StarHeart story about the art of saying *thank you*:

The StarHeart Angel Brigade
has an important message for you,
Read each word carefully
to know what to do.

These special words of wisdom
are for everyone young and old,
Each time you say thank you
the words are like a "pot of gold."

Once you get the habit
of saying thanks for e-v-e-r-y thing,
Your life will have more zest
and definitely a lot more zing!

Saying thank you doesn't always
have to make total sense,
Say it often, say it out loud
it really works in the present tense!

Expressing thank you isn't just
when "mind your manners" is said,
Saying thank you can begin
the moment you get out of bed!

Your body will love you
each time you recognize,
All the neat stuff that it does
like seeing "eye to eye."

There are all those little things
that lots of people do,
How often do you take the time
to say how much it means to you?

Say thank you to the birds
say it to the bees,
Say it gratefully especially when
you "see the forest through the trees!"

Be thankful for the raindrops
and loud and roaring thunder,
Now this may somewhat surprise you
say thank you even for a "blunder!"

In case you haven't noticed
saying thank you requires no special tools,
Remember the first rule is
that's just it...there are no rules!

Simply put, it's plain to see
saying thank you is an art,
Try it now and see what happens
when you say thank you with all your heart!

The full-length version of THANKYOUOLOGY is packed with more than a hundred *thank you* ideas, positive psychology research, inspirational stories and personal anecdotes. Written in what I call a "conversational textbook" style, this how-to-book is divided into three parts—basic tools, applications and advanced practice. To turn *the talk* into *the walk*, the Notes section at the end of each chapter is filled with action-step activities, suggestions for the work-place, references, resources and *thank you* quotes.

Even though the *Chicago Manual of Style* states other-wise, I have deliberately indented, skipped a line between paragraphs and widened the margins for notes. The more you make this information yours, the more you will integrate and own it for yourself.

Before getting started, there are a few more points I would like to make.

First, THANKYOUOLOGY is about the infinite power of saying *thank you* with thoughts, words and actions. Some people may specifically say *thank you* to God, Lord or Jesus while others express their gratitude to Jehovah, Spirit, the Divine Mind or other possibilities too numerous to list. Out of respect for all faiths and spiritual beliefs, there is no religious reference attached to the words, *thank you*. It is for you to determine who or what you wish to acknowledge, if you choose to do so.

Next, I would like to say *thank you* to the authors of children's books because many of their messages motivate me to expand my thinking. After reading *I'm In Charge of Celebrations* by Byrd Baylor, I decided to celebrate New Year's Eve on the last day of January since I always thought the holiday was just too close to Christmas. *The True Story of the Three Little Pigs* by A. Wolf teaches me there's always another perspective, and *Caretakers of Wonder* by Cooper Edens stirs my imagination with ideas to help keep the world magical.

Finally, while THANKYOUOLOGY may appear to be a book for adults, it is great for children and teenagers too. So grownups, please share it with the younger folks in your life. The sooner they know the importance of saying *thank you*, beyond when "mind your manners" is said, the sooner they have access to a valuable tool that helps them take charge of their life.

Now, the question is: Are you ready to take charge of your health, relationships, the manifestation of your dreams and more? Are you eager to be a THANKYOUOLOGIST and create a most magnificent way to live? Great, because I believe THANKYOUOLOGY will definitely transform your life, since practicing the art of saying *thank you* certainly has transformed mine.

Yes, indeed!

*These special words of wisdom
are for everyone young and old,
Each time you say thank you
the words are like a "pot of gold."*

How Thoughts, Words and Actions Create Your Life

Words. Words. Words. How important are they?

Combinations of words tell us stories, convey our feelings, urge us to buy something, persuade us to think a certain way, and give us instructions. Words are also the catalyst of our actions.

It is said that everything begins with a thought. It has also been said that we think thousands of thoughts a day—as many as 50,000 to 60,000 of them. To understand how the words, *thank you*, are like a "pot of gold," a look at our thoughts is a good place to start.

According to the dictionary definition, thoughts are the product of our thinking. While modern day philosophers may tell us that we think too much or spend too much time in our heads, "positive psychologists" tell us that what we think and how often we think it has a direct impact on our lives.

There are many synonyms for the word thought: belief, brain wave, concept, idea, inspiration, notion, opinion, philosophy, reflection or theory. And, there are many ways to describe thoughts such as angry, crazy, delightful, happy, intriguing, negative, pensive, positive, and...well, I think you get the picture.

Researching this topic, I found people have been pondering thoughts since the beginning of time.

Buddha (563 BC—483 BC), founder of Buddhism stated: "What we are today comes from our thoughts of yesterday, and our present thoughts build our life of tomorrow. Our life is the creation of our mind."

In Proverbs it is written: "For as a man thinketh in his heart, so is he." Psychotherapist, Dr. Wayne Dyer's version of this biblical statement is, "I think and that is all that I am."

Born in Switzerland a year after Columbus discovered America, a man named Paracelsus offered: "Thoughts are free and subject to no rule. On them rests the freedom of man, and they tower above the light of nature...creating a new heaven, a new firmament, a new source of energy from which new arts flow."

Ralph Waldo Emerson said, "Great men are they who see that spiritual thought is stronger than any material force, that thoughts rule the world."

Today, inspirations on this topic include: "You are what you think" and "Attitude determines altitude."

At the age of five, I was introduced to the idea that our thoughts have power when I attended a Unity church in Pomona, California. During Lent, while my friends were giving up gum or something else that to me seemed simple to do for 40 days, I was encouraged to give up negative thinking. I must admit that when I was around my friends, I wasn't always the first to volunteer that I gave up negative thoughts for Lent. The idea that thoughts determine our life experiences didn't have near the popularity that it has today.

You may be feeling that it's good enough to think positive thoughts a majority of the time. After hearing a motivational speaker point out that a majority can be as little as 50.1 percent, I looked at how that translates mathematically.

If we use 50,000 thoughts for the calculation, 50.1 percent is 25,050 leaving the remaining 24,950 thoughts up for grabs. The way I see it, the power of positive thinking is diluted if nearly half the time is spent thinking negatively.

Speaking of counting thoughts, Geshe Michael Roach, the author of *The Diamond Cutter: The Buddha on Managing Your Business and Your Life*, tells a story about the Buddhists of Tibet who used a bag of black and white pebbles to keep track of their thoughts.

I find it fascinating that stones were used to sum up thoughts and actions throughout the day. White stones signified good thoughts or kind behavior toward someone, and black stones meant negative thoughts or actions.

According to the story, the left pocket of their robe was for the white stones and the right pocket was for the black stones. Throughout the day, stones were placed in both the right and left pockets depending on whether thoughts and actions were positive or negative.

Before going to bed, the pebbles in each pocket were counted to keep score of their actions during the day.

I am not suggesting that we use this ancient practice or any other method to keep track of our thoughts. That takes too much time. I do have a suggestion about pebbles taken from a story I read years ago: Think of negative thoughts as a pebble on the ground. Amongst many others, it is small and insignificant. If you take that pebble and put it right in front of your eye, even the tiniest little pebble prevents you from seeing anything else. This is a good metaphor to remember.

Today there are writers, speakers, religious leaders, psychologists and many others talking about the power of our thoughts. I think the Peace Pilgrim said it best when she was quoted as saying: "If you realized how powerful your thoughts are, you would never think a negative thought."

For those who prefer visual proof, Dr. Masaru Emoto uses sophisticated photography to show the impact of thoughts on water molecules. His self-published books, *Messages from Water* and *The Hidden Messages in Water*, feature convincing photographs that show the effects of specific thoughts (both negative and positive) on water molecules.

Dr. Emoto's research was used in the movie, *What the Bleep Do I Know?* In a scene, Marlee Matlin, who stars as Amanda, is in a museum looking at a photo exhibit. Each poster-size photograph shows the molecular structure of water when it was in a bottle labeled with different words such as love, *thank you* and hate.

The camera follows Amanda as she carefully looks at each of the photographs. In the posters displaying water bottles with positive words, the molecules are green and blue. When she sees the photograph of a water bottle with the word hate on it, the colors of the molecules are harsh reds and black. As she is staring at this poster with a look of disbelief, a man appears from behind the poster and poses the question: "If thoughts can do this to water, what can they do to you?"

I think now is a good time to quote Frank Outlaw's statement: "Watch your thoughts, they become your words."

In the book, *The Four Agreements* by Don Miguel Ruiz, he states that the first of the four agreements is the most important—be impeccable with your word. According to Ruiz, "Through the word, you express your creative power. It is through the word that you manifest everything."

Recognizing the power of words, there are some words and phrases I believe could be changed or eliminated to improve what we manifest in our lives. For example:

I grew up hearing and saying, "That makes me sick." Not surprising that I was frequently sick. When I became conscious of using the phrase, the first step I took to eliminate it from my speech was to say, "That is sickening." Eventually, I was able to drop all reference to sickness when I talk about my feelings.

A co-worker at a job often described people as "a pain in the neck." Interesting how she was always going to the chiropractor for adjustments to her neck!

What about the reference to "pain in the butt?" Is that really worth affirming? Also, give some thought to whether you want to say that something "kills you."

Another popular phrase is: "I would give my right arm to have such and such." Personally I won't trade any of my body parts for something. I would rather say *thank you* and get it that way!

Hearing someone say, "I am bad" or "I am so stupid," prompts me to suggest replacing the negative adjective with a positive one. It is my belief that whatever follows the words, "I am" is what is.

Well-worn phrases worth eliminating are: "to die for," "small token" and "I can't *thank you* enough." I would much rather "live for" something wouldn't you? Why do we have to describe any gesture of gratitude as small? I believe we are all capable of expressing our thanks with heartfelt sincerity and appreciation. Why disrespect ourselves and say that we can't?

When someone repeatedly exclaims, "I can't believe it," I say believe what you can create with light and love and celebrate it with a most enthusiastic, THANK YOU!

Now that we have thought about thoughts and talked about words, that's my cue to continue with Frank Outlaw's quote: "Watch your words for they become your actions." Mathematically, it could be said that thoughts plus words equal actions. In THANKYOUOLOGY terms, that means: *Thank you* thoughts plus *thank you* words equal *thank you* actions—the definition of a gratitude consciousness also known as your "pot of gold."

In The *Alchemy of Gratitude*, Karol Avalon writes: "Gratitude is a conscious choice to focus on life's blessings rather than on its shortcomings. In this understanding, the practice of gratitude is a way of life. Every moment is filled with opportunities to fill our consciousness with feelings of gratefulness, thankfulness and appreciation. From the littlest flower we see in the garden to the traffic jam on the way to work, we can choose to be grateful."

Books are packed with words of wisdom about gratitude and motivational speakers around the world declare the countless benefits of being thankful. There is definitely no shortage of quotes or commentary assuring us that choosing to "focus on life's blessings rather than on its shortcomings" is the best choice to make.

How do you focus on life's blessings rather than its shortcomings? How do you create the optimistic life you want to live? It is said that computers perform at the level of their programming; the same is true with your mind. It is the quality of your programming (thoughts) that determines what you experience. Thus, what you want to attract in your life can be programmed with your thoughts .

Since my personal mission statement is to live a lifestyle of simple elegance, I believe that using the power of *thank you* is the simplest and most effective way to focus my thoughts. The next three chapters give you powerful ideas to do this with the use of *thank you* rhymes, affirmations and the Gold Star *Thank You* Journal. For now, I will conclude this chapter with the reminder:

> *You have the power to think*
> *you have the power to say,*
> *You have the power to act*
> *make it thank you all the way!*

Now it's time for lights, camera and THANKYOU-OLOGY action!

Activities

1. Observe your word choices for a day. Have fun noticing what you say and see if you would like to say it differently. For example, telling someone: "Don't forget to take out the trash," could be said: "*Thank you for remembering to take out the trash.*" Two things are accomplished by saying it this way—the request is stated in the positive and you are already thanking the person for doing the task.

    List five of your word choice discoveries here.

    1. _____

    2. _____

    3. _____

    4. _____

    5. _____

2. There are Positive Psychology researchers and many others studying the benefits of gratitude and identifying gratitude role models. Following are a few leaders in the field:

    • Dr. Michael McCullough, University of Miami has

written *The Psychology of Gratitude*. His research is dedicated to three areas—forgiveness and revenge, gratitude, and religion and spirituality.

- Dr. Robert Emmons, University of California, Davis, is a researcher in personality psychology, the psychology of emotion and religion. His primary interests are in the psychology of gratitude and the psychology of personal goals, and how each is related to positive psychological processes, including happiness, well-being and personality integration.

- Dr. Darren Weissman has written *The Power of Infinite Love and Gratitude*, applying Emmons' findings directly to physical health.

At the Workplace

Be a role model in your workplace about the power of words. Pay attention to your emails, written correspondence and what you say to others. Whenever possible, share your perspective about words and encourage others to join you in focusing more on the positive than the negative.

References & Resources

Books

Melody Beattie
  Gratitude

Masaru Emoto
  Messages from Water
  The Hidden Messages in Water

Geshe Michael Roach
  The Diamond Cutter: The Buddha on Managing Your Business and Your Life

Don Miguel Ruiz
  The Four Agreements

M.J. Ryan
  Attitudes of Gratitude

Peace Pilgrim

From 1953 to 1981, she walked more than 25,000 miles back and forth across the United States carrying her only possessions in the pocket of her blue tunic. This woman is my role model for detachment which she said took 14 years to achieve. After that, what freedom!

If you have not heard of the Peace Pilgrim, treat yourself to a little time on the internet or better yet, obtain a copy of the book by the same name. While it is not an autobiography, her own words were transcribed from recordings, conversations and what others had to say about how she touched their lives. How fitting that my mom, who hitchhiked from Central City, Nebraska to California in 1940, introduced me to the inspiring story about the Peace Pilgrim. *Thank you, mom!*

Websites

What The Bleep Do I Know? (movie)
www.whatthebleep.com

Thank You Quotes

Alan Cohen: *If you took one tenth of the energy you invest in criticism and converted it to gratitude, one's life would improve a hundredfold.*

Meister Eckhart: *If the only prayer you said in your whole life was thank you that would suffice.*

Obaa-san: *Every thought we think, every word we speak, and every act we carry out generates ripples of Universal energy producing effects that will return to us in kind.*

Anwar Sadat: *He who cannot change the fabric of his thoughts will never be able to change reality.*

*Once you get the habit
of saying thanks for e-v-e-r-y thing,
Your life will have more zest
and definitely a lot more zing!*

How to Create *Thank You* Rhymes

Habit. Synonyms are pattern, tradition, tendency, preference, practice.

Zest. Defined as enthusiasm, gusto, passion.

Question: How do you initiate the habit of training your mind to achieve a life filled with "zest and definitely a lot more zing?" The answer starts with your thoughts. To be completely alive, full of enthusiasm and passionate for life, it is necessary to be in the present moment with your thoughts—the powerful energy behind your words and actions.

Next question: Are you living in the present moment?

According to Eknath Easwaran: "If we could watch our thoughts, we would find that instead of being here and now, our attention is constantly wandering everywhere and everywhere else—to the past, to the future, to the Never-Never Lands that reality has never visited."

Scientific studies report that up to 40 percent of our attention is fixed on the past and projections into the future account for as much as another 40 percent. According to the Buddha, we are bankrupt to handle the present when our mind is not paying attention. When we are thinking about past hurts or wrongdoings, or thinking about future concerns, we are unable to effectively handle anything in the present moment.

American psychologist, William James, remarked in a *Vogue* magazine article: "The faculty of voluntarily bringing back a wandering attention, over and over again, is the very root of judgment, character and will." From this statement, it could be said that good judgment, strong character and a positive will are much more desirable than the results of wandering attention, confusion and lack of focus.

Living in the present affords you the benefit of having at your beck and call every possible resource your mind can provide. Spending "think time" in the past or the future robs your mind of this potential. If your mind doesn't have all it needs to function in the moment, you compromise your ability to greet the day with gusto, deal with challenges that may arise or even celebrate the successes you achieve.

There are countless examples and stories that demonstrate the power of razor-sharp focus and attention in the present moment. Books are filled with them! My favorite role model is watching Tiger Woods. He simply gives all of his attention to that little white ball and where he aims for it to land. The training he had as a young child, and commitment he makes to this sport, gives spectators around the world quite a treat! *Thank you*, Tiger.

How do you train your attention to be in the present moment? Develop mindfulness? For centuries, meditation has been a practice taught by many religions and mystical traditions. Are there other methods for use throughout the day to focus your attention, to be in the "here and now?" YES!

In the philosophy of THANKYOUOLOGY, there is a basic tool that focuses the attention and also activates the practice of saying *thank you* for E-V-E-R-Y-T-H-I-N-G. It is easy. It is fun. It is powerful. What is it? *Thank you* rhymes!

I love using *thank you* rhymes to train my brain to think and say *thank you*. With this habit, *thank you* rhymes run through my head like excited children on Christmas morning. They dart here, giggle there and sometimes sound like they are screaming at the top of their lungs. What began as an entertaining mental exercise to focus my attention on the present moment, has become a very powerful *thank you* tool.

What I am suggesting is for you to create *thank you* rhymes about anything that comes into your mind. For example, this is what just popped into mine:

> *Thank you* for days with nothing to do
> *Thank you* for girlfriends named Sue.

You may have noticed that *thank you* rhymes don't have to make any kind of sense. That means you can put unrelated thoughts together such as:

> *Thank you* for Hollywood's night of Academy Awards
> *Thank you* for basketball hoops and fast skateboards.

Or, use *thank you* rhymes to express one particular thought such as this:

> *Thank you* for my *thank you* rhymes with ease
> *Thank you* for a quick response, if you please.

Say this rhyme a few times if you need help getting started. If you have a critical parent somewhere inside, please tell it to take a break. The key is to let your imagination run wild, and when you do, you will discover that your mind has to be in the present moment to accomplish this mental activity.

Thank you rhymes are easy even for the poetically challenged. In the beginning, write them down to help you get the hang of it. Eventually they will become more automatic and just bubble out of your thoughts. Here is how to get started:

1. Think of a word—any word. How about jello?

2. Play around with words that rhyme with jello such as mellow, yellow, fellow or bellow.

3. Pick one of the rhyming words and put them together. For example:

Thank you for luscious green jello
Thank you for the color yellow.

Or...

Thank you for yellow jello
Thank you for sounds which are mellow.

Need a little more help? Here are some *thank you* rhymes to practice with by filling in the missing word. Suggested answers are in the chapter Notes.

Thank you for my heart open wide
Thank you for my funny _____.

Thank you for holding my hand
Thank you for every particle of _____.

Thank you for the ability to remember
Thank you for the month of _____.

Thank you for radiant health
Thank you for prosperity and _____.

Thank you for all my dreams that come true
Thank you for the question, "Who _____?"

Thank you for the birds and bees
Thank you for my sturdy _____.

Thank you for healthy fingernails
Thank you for cats and puppy dog _____.

Thank you for arms that give lots of hugs
Thank you for those cute little _____.

The rhythm of the *thank you* rhymes works just like songs—once you hear them, they repeat over and over again in your head. Without much effort, I find myself saying favorite *thank you* rhymes all day long. What starts as a one or two-minute activity easily grows into a ten or fifteen-minute practice, particularly if I am out walking or have some waiting time. Believing the possibilities are endless, my collection of *thank you* rhymes starts on page 173 to give you ideas for creating your own. *Thank you, Marlene, for categorizing them!*

The fun of saying *thank you* for E-V-E-R-Y-T-H-I-N-G with *thank you* rhymes has a way of animating your thoughts in general, which gives you other rewards. It is said that the more you live in your imagination, the more you are able to piece together seemingly impossible ideas to create new possibilities.

Geshe Michael Roach offers: "Those who write poetry can find original solutions to problems pretty easily." I have found this free-form style of thinking definitely fuels a fertile mental playground for creative problem solving. And, with a light-hearted spirit on the inside, here is what can happen on the outside:

1. Your life has more zest and a lot more zing!

2. You smile more.

3. People smile back at you.

4. You say *thank you* to people more often.

5. People say *thank you* more often to you.

6. Did I mention that your life has more zest and zing?

There are so many reasons to develop the habit of creating *thank you* rhymes. I look forward to hearing your stories about using them. And, in the next chapter, be ready to discover how a different kind of *thank you* rhyme has the potential to focus your will and manifest your desires. With all of this potential, that is why I am cheering you on to great success with your *thank you* rhymes because:

You have the creative capability
to focus your mind with ease,
Thank you rhymes keep you in the now
just like laughter and a sneeze!

....*Notes*

Activities

1. The suggested answers for the fill in *thank you* rhymes are:

    - *Thank you* for my funny side.

    - *Thank you* for every particle of sand.

    - *Thank you* for the month of December.

    - *Thank you* for prosperity and wealth.

    - *Thank you* for the saying, "who knew?"

    - *Thank you* for my sturdy knees.

    - *Thank you* for cats and puppy dog tails.

    - *Thank you* for those cute little bugs.

2. See how many times throughout the day you can say *thank you*. Remember, it doesn't have to be FOR anything. This is about training your mind to think and say *thank you*.

3. Create a collection of your *thank you* rhymes. There is space on pages 190-192 to get you started. Put your favorites on sticky notes and scatter them everywhere. Teach others about *thank you* rhymes and share them with one another.

At the Workplace

A great way to see the positive things about your job is to write *thank you* rhymes. You have a lot of subject matter—your workspace, co-workers, supervisor, responsibilities, hours, pay, benefits, company management and anything else that comes to mind such as being close to home, provision of child care, social opportunities and education benefits.

Self-employed? *Thank you* rhymes work for you too!

Not so thrilled about your job? You can improve it or take a step toward a new one by writing *thank you* rhymes.

Thank You Quotes

Maya Angelou: *I don't even say what I am thankful for. Generally, I just say, thank you, thank you, thank you.*

Thomas Erskine: *A grateful heart is a 24-hour religion.*

William A. Ward: *God gave you a gift of 86,400 seconds today. Have you used one to say thank you?*

*Saying thank you doesn't always
have to make total sense,
Say it often, say it out loud
it really works in the present tense!*

How to Affirm *Thank You*

Affirmations. What are they?

Affirmations are verbal visualizations, declared with positive intentions and stated in the present tense. With the belief that affirmations work, affirmations give you the ability to take personal responsibility for your life—anytime, anywhere.

In order to use affirmations in the art of saying *thank you*, it is important to understand how and why affirmations work.

Affirmations work on the subconscious level using concise statements to replace negative beliefs with positive, self-nurturing attitudes. Negative beliefs include any kind of criticism or destructive judgment of yourself, others or circumstances. Reversing negative self-talk with positive affirmations is a powerful personal development tool.

And why do affirmations work? They work because the mind reacts to how it is programmed. If the programming (self-talk) is negative, the lack of self-esteem immobilizes and keeps a person stuck in repetitive patterns of behavior. Pessimism, depression and lifeless emotions are also common side effects of negative self-talk.

Just as negative thoughts have the power to create dysfunction, positive thoughts or affirmations have the unlimited potential to create what we want in any given moment. Want to be happy? Affirm happiness! Want to feel good about yourself? Affirm productive attributes! Desire to have success in your relationships, business, or ??? Plain and simple: Affirm it!

Affirmations that begin with "I am" keep you, and the intention, in the present tense. Starting an affirmation with "I can" or "I will" suspends the intention as if it is something in the future rather than in "the now." You have the power to determine your truth in any given moment. When you choose to be positive in your thinking, "I am" is the passageway to infinite possibilities for you and what you experience in your life. Examples of positive affirmations are:

I am great	I am talented
I am wonderful	I am artistic
I am rich	I am understanding
I am love	I am competent
I am peace	I am creative
I am successful	I am dazzling

In addition to the subject/verb combination of "I am," many other verbs are used for positive affirmations such as:

I choose	I have	I love
I create	I enjoy	I receive
I express	I know	I believe

Believing in the power of affirmations, the art of saying *thank you* takes this mental tool one step further by creating affirmations to both declare the intention and give thanks for it. Now you have an extraordinary method for manifesting desires and strengthening your will.

How do you use *thank you* affirmations? Even though books are filled with suggestions, I think it is best to craft your own, tailored exactly to your intentions.

To get started, pick out something that is important to you. Think about the qualities you want to feel or experience. With those thoughts, make a positive affirmation. For example: I create innovative marketing strategies that are successful at my job. The added octane is affirming the intention and saying *thank you* for it as if the intention has already happened. Now, that same affirmation is: *Thank you* for the successful innovative marketing strategies that I create at my job. That is what I call a *thank you* affirmation.

Throughout the day, use *thank you* affirmations to help you with anything from finding an item to "finding your way." The key is to act as if whatever you need or want is already yours in that moment. With practice, you will often find the response to *thank you* affirmations is spontaneous. Finding a parking space when it appears there are none is a perfect example. When I am on approach, I say *thank you* to the person who is vacating the space where I will park, and I say *thank you* for the parking space itself. The double *thank you* works every time!

I am constantly using *thank you* affirmations. To me, they are *thank you* rhymes with intention. And like you, throughout the day, I have hundreds of intentions—to find this, fix that, follow through on whatever, or feel such and such. The list just keeps on going. And, *thank you* affirmations are right there in the middle of it all.

When you use *thank you* affirmations for the little things, you gain confidence to use *thank you* affirmations for all your desires regardless of how big or impossible they may seem. In addition to thinking or saying *thank you* affirmations for what I call, "the big ticket" items, writing *thank you* affirmations strengthens your resolve and belief in the intention. Here are a few guidelines to help you:

1. Decide what you want. Be very clear, very specific.

2. Think about your desire. What are the qualities? How does it feel? How will you feel receiving it? Describe the feelings in detail using "I am" statements.

3. Believe that your desire already exists. Talk about it with others in the present tense.

4. Give thanks for your desire. Write it, say it, sing it, dance to it. Say *thank you* constantly for what you want, believing you already have it.

5. Let your desire go. When those fears and *what ifs* come up, say *thank you* and keep on keeping on.

In the spring of 2007, I anticipated using these guidelines to manifest a place to live during the summer. I had been staying at my mom's house getting it ready to sell after my sister and I relocated her to a wonderful assisted-living residence. Even though I disliked the hot summer temperatures where she lived, it appeared that was where I would live until the house was sold.

I was so busy with my mom's affairs that I didn't write my *thank you* affirmations for a place to live during the summer. Instead, I just remember saying *thank you* for a cooler place to live, and in my humorous way, commented that Laguna Beach would be nice. That's it!

Two weeks later, I received a call from dear friends who asked if I would like to stay in their Laguna Beach home for the months of June through August while they went to their summer home in Idaho. Affectionately called the "tree house," this is where I had the privilege of writing the first draft of THANKYOUOLOGY. What a gift to live in a quiet, serene area of Laguna Beach referred to as Top of the World. That is how I felt when I was hiking in the hills minutes from their door or gazing at the ocean when I needed a break from writing. *Thank you*, Jack and Kathie!

While I was writing THANKYOUOLOGY, I practiced its principles with every opportunity. Two stories that may seem insignificant stand out because they prove how easily and effortlessly *thank you* affirmations work when appearances may seem otherwise.

One morning, while I was waiting at the bus stop to go to the beach for Laughter Yoga, I realized I had forgotten my bottle of water. It was very early and there wasn't a soul in sight. I said a *thank you* affirmation for a bottle of water since I did not have enough time to go back and get one.

Within minutes, a lady opened her garage door to load some things in her car. I walked over and asked if she had a bottle of water which she did. As I was saying *thank you*, the bus arrived and I hopped on board smiling at how quickly my *thank you* affirmation was answered.

Another time I was heading for that same bus stop when I noticed I didn't put lotion on my legs. May sound a bit silly, I said a *thank you* affirmation for lotion anyway!

Typically, there was never anyone else waiting at the bus stop. On this particular day, another lady was already there. We greeted each other with a smile, and then moments later she reached into her purse and pulled out a bottle of lotion. YES, a bottle of lotion!

She looked at me and asked if I would like some lotion. Of course I said, "Yes!" I don't know which was more exciting—having her offer me the lotion or the idea of telling you this story! It just shows what happens when you have fun with *thank you* affirmations. And, she encouraged me to use as much as I wanted—a confirmation that our needs are abundantly answered.

Is it coincidence? Is it luck? I choose to believe it is the power of *thank you* affirmations that keeps my attention focused on the present—a great basic tool for the art of saying *thank you*.

Feeling that you aren't creative to come up with *thank you* affirmations? Start with saying *thank you* for affirmations that work for you. Then, look around, listen to the words in songs, read poems—even the dialogue in a movie can inspire a *thank you* affirmation such as one that came to me from the movie, *Dan in Real Life*. The main character, Dan, suggested: "Instead of teaching our children to plan their lives, we should teach them to plan to be surprised." From that line I created the affirmation: *Thank you* for delightful surprises in my life beyond my imagination.

Karen Drucker is a remarkable singer-songwriter who claims when she discovered the power of positive affirmations, her music and her life changed. To me, many of her songs are *thank you* affirmations put to music such as the chant: *Thank you for this day spirit/Thank you for this day*.

The lyrics in another song of hers offer a great affirmation for financial abundance: *Money is coming to me easily and effortlessly/Money is coming to me*. When the song ends, there is the cha-ching sound of a cash register that always makes me giggle. From the lyrics, I created this affirmation: *Thank you* for money that comes to me easily and effortlessly.

From the song, *Silent Night*, I say *thank you* for "all is calm." Terry Cole Whittaker's book, *What You Think of Me is None of My Business*, gave me this affirmation: *Thank you* for my belief that what someone thinks of me is none of my business.

One of my most magical *thank you* affirmations came from the advice a friend gave me about making decisions. She told me to always ask myself if the choice thrills me. That is how I arrived at this affirmation: *Thank you* for experiences that thrill me! This next story is a great example of what I receive as a result.

While I was finalizing THANKYOUOLOGY (as if that wasn't thrilling enough), a Hollywood casting director called to see if I was available to be a background actor in a highly confidential science fiction film. It was a thrill just going to the studio a couple of times for wardrobe fittings. The action-packed scenes were exciting and so was the thrill of being used as a stand-in. The biggest thrill was watching a famous director and hundreds of crew creating what is sure to be a blockbuster film.

I love saying *thank you* for the thrill of it all and you will too. When you live in the moment with *thank you* affirmations, you are able to respond to guidance and direction that may feel like intuition or a hunch. Being mentally available to this guidance, you suddenly turn down a certain aisle in the parking lot or make a call that gives you a life-changing message. The more you use *thank you* affirmations, the more you experience the unlimited possibilities of keeping your attention and intentions in the present moment.

Now that *thank you* rhymes and affirmations have been explained, there is one more tool in the basics of saying *thank you*. Before moving to the next chapter describing how to use a *thank you* journal, I have these words of encouragement for you:

> *Thank you affirmations*
> *they really are the best,*
> *Once you build the practice*
> *you will hardly take a rest.*
>
> *Use them for everything*
> *whatever you desire or need,*
> *Stay focused in the here and now*
> *I know you will succeed!*

.... *Notes*

Activities

1. Use *thank you* affirmations in art projects by capturing your favorites with creative photography, drawings or watercolors. Make collages, embed words in a ceramic piece or paint a *thank you* affirmation on a wooden plaque. They are excellent reminders for you or they can be given to others as gifts.

2. Use *thank you* affirmations to set goals, activate dreams or anything else your heart desires. Create *thank you* affirmations and use them daily. Here are category suggestions to get you started: Professional Pursuits, Relationships and Personal Goals.

3. Make a list of your favorite "I am" statements to use when you hear negative self talk. Examples are:

    I am creative and exciting. My clients love me!

    I always have what I need at the moment I need it.

    I am talented, intelligent and powerful.

    I am making a difference.

    I am enthusiastic about people and about life.

    I am joyful and fun-loving.

At the Workplace

Identify something about your job that you don't like. Create a *thank you* affirmation changing the focus from negative to positive. You can do this for anything—*thank you* for the windows, color of the walls, décor, furniture, comfy desk chair, plants inside, plants outside, airy feeling, special co-workers, the hours of work and/or short commute.

References & Resources

Websites

Karen Drucker
www.karendrucker.com

Thank You Quotes

G.K. Chesterton: *I would maintain that thanks are the highest form of thought, and that gratitude is happiness doubled by wonder.*

William Shakespeare: *I can no other answer make, but, thanks, and thanks.*

*Expressing thank you isn't just
when "mind your manners" is said,
Saying thank you can begin
the moment you get out of bed!*

How to Use a *Thank You* Journal

Thankful. Are you saying *thank you* "the moment you get out of bed?"

Della Reese, singer and star of television's *Touched by An Angel*, asked a similar question at the beginning of her church service in November 1997. The question was: "When you woke up this morning, did you give thanks for being alive?"

"When you woke up this morning," she continued, "did you give thanks that your heart was working and that you were breathing?" Next she asked: "Did you give thanks that you could think about getting out of bed and actually do it?"

After each question, she looked at the audience long and hard. Then she launched into a humorous commentary about giving thanks for the ability to get out of bed with special attention to the knees. To this day, I always say *thank you* to my knees when I get out of bed in the morning.

It was this story, and my love for gold stars when I was an elementary school teacher, that inspired me to create the Gold Star *Thank You* Journal. Designed to focus the mind on saying *thank you* first thing in the morning, the Gold Star *Thank You* Journal consists of three activities:

1. Making a list of *thank you* statements.

2. Creating *thank you* affirmations.

3. Giving out gold stars at the end of the day.

Why do I call it the Gold Star *Thank You* Journal? When I was teaching, I created the Magic Star Fairy, an imaginary helper who rewarded students for every positive step. There were stars on the blackboard, stars on the bulletin boards, stars on their papers and stars on their desks when she checked for neatness. It was a star-studded classroom and the kids knew they were special.

There was a point system for both independent achievements and working together with their classmates that ultimately earned each student a gold-star T-shirt. I figured star-studded T-shirts would last longer than a piece of candy. You can bet my students were quite proud to wear their shirts and show their friends on the playground. That's how we all should feel about our accomplishments.

When I thought about creating a tool to focus my mind on thankfulness the moment I woke up, I knew it would include gold stars. Mentally I love to give gold stars to myself and verbally I enjoy giving them to others when I say, "a gold star for you."

As a child, I loved receiving stars on my schoolwork and at the end of a piano lesson. I have never outgrown my love for stars. As an adult I have wondered: *Why did we stop giving out the gold stars?* I think the answer lies somewhere in the tendency to only acknowledge the final outcome rather than recognizing each step it takes to get there.

To use an analogy, when I was teaching, it was frustrating for me to grade math problems as either a right or wrong answer. What about all of the correct calculations for a long division or a multiplication problem even if the final answer was wrong? I felt it was important to acknowledge what was correct rather than mark the problem wrong because of an incorrect answer.

That's a little background on the Gold Star *Thank You* Journal, now for how to use it.

In the morning…

1. Begin your quiet time using slow, deliberate breaths.

2. Once you feel centered, turn to your journal page and fill in the date—helpful for reflecting on your progress.

3. Next, write what you are thankful for—at least five things. Keep it simple. This step is designed to get your *thank you* wheels in gear.

4. Finally, create your own *thank you* affirmations (Chapter 3). This is your opportunity to affirm anything you desire—health, wealth and happiness are popular choices! If something is bothering you, write a *thank you* affirmation for the specific feelings that you want to have, and there is sure to be a shift. Examples of *thank you* affirmations are:

   For health
   Thank you for being free of pain.
   Thank you for breathing easier today.
   Thank you for my eyes that see so clearly.

   For wealth
   Thank you for the money to repay a loan.
   Thank you for extra cash to use on vacation.
   Thank you for my child's school tuition.

   For happiness
   Thank you for more than I can imagine.
   Thank you for peace and serenity in my heart.
   Thank you for dazzling delights that thrill me.

In the evening…

5. Return to your journal before bedtime and give out the gold stars. This is where you acknowledge every step of success. Recognize the slightest thing that was different or changed. See what showed up as a result of your *thank you* affirmations. Pay attention to the synchronicity that you just can't explain.

Even if you think you don't have time to write in the morning or at night, I urge you to give the Gold Star *Thank You* Journal a try for 30 days. Once you develop the habit, you will find it's a most effective way to create the kind of day you want. Journal pages for a month start on page 141. For extended use, make photocopies of the blank journal pages, design your own or choose one of the recommended journal books listed in the chapter Notes.

For those who just can't make the writing habit stick, say your *thank you* list as you are in the shower, making coffee, exercising or running out the door. At night in bed, take a few minutes and give out the gold stars. Before going to sleep, think *thank you* thoughts and for sure, it's sweet dreams!

The benefits of using the Gold Star *Thank You* Journal are unlimited. With time and focus, things just start happening differently when you write your daily *thank you* list and affirmations. Together, these routines reinforce your intention to direct your life in a balanced and productive manner.

The Gold Star *Thank You* Journal completes the four basic tools in the art of saying *thank you*. For review, they are:

Be conscious of your thoughts
words and actions too,
Create thank you affirmations
for everything you do.

Practice the fun of writing
more than one thank you rhyme,
Acknowledge each step you take
with gold stars--especially at night time!

Now it's time for part two—applying the art of saying *thank you!*

....*Notes*

Activities

1. Consider an art class to expand your exploration of gratitude and write about your discoveries in your Gold Star *Thank You* Journal.

2. Get together with friends and form a *thank you* journal group to share ideas for affirmations along with goals and dreams. Give each other gold stars for every accomplishment toward achieving your heart's desires.

3. At a party or craft store, purchase gold stars in various sizes or make your own. Put them in special places as reminders to give gold stars to YOU!

4. Have fun with acronyms for the kind of "star" you are such as: **S**omeone **T**errific **A**nd **R**adiant! An environmental star is **S**omeone **T**hat **A**lways **R**ecycles! There are many more possibilities...just let your imagination go!

At the Workplace

The Gold Star *Thank You* Journal works at the office too! As soon as you arrive, take a few minutes to write what you are thankful for about your job. Create a *thank you* affirmation for your day and write it down. I use my Outlook calendar to note my gold stars at the end of each day. This also helps me look back over the week and see everything that I accomplished.

References & Resources

Gratitude Journals

Sarah Ban Breathnach
The Simple Abundance Journal of Gratitude

Melody Beattie
> *The Language of Letting Go Journal: A Meditation Book and Journal for Daily Reflection*

James Bluestein
> *Daily Riches: A Gratitude Journal*

Franz Kafka
> *Abundantly Simple: Every Woman's Gratitude Journal*

M. J. Ryan
> *Attitude of Gratitude Journal*

Thank You **Quotes**

Dr. Joe Dispenza: *I wake up in the morning and I consciously create my day the way I want it to happen. Now sometimes, because my mind is examining all the things that I need to get done, it takes me a little bit to settle down and get to the point of where I'm actually intentionally creating my day. (From the film, What The Bleep Do I Know?)*

Abraham-Hicks: *Every time you appreciate something, every time you praise something, every time you feel good about something, you are telling the Universe, more of this, please. You need never make another verbal statement of this intent, and if you are mostly in a state of appreciation, all good things will flow to you.*

Geshe Michael Roach: *People that fail to succeed with the principles invariably fail for one of two reasons: They don't follow them over a good amount of time, or they don't follow them very well.*

Adapted from the Internet...Everyday Thanksgiving: *Even though I clutch my blanket and growl when the alarm rings, thank you that I can hear. There are many who are deaf.*

Even though I keep my eyes closed against the morning lights as long as possible, thank you that I can see. Many are blind.

Even though I huddle in my bed and put off rising, thank you that I have the strength to rise. There are many who are bedridden.

Even though the first hour of my day is hectic, when socks are lost, toast is burned and tempers are short and my children are so loud, thank you for my family. There are many who are lonely.

Even though our breakfast table never looks like the pictures in magazines and the menu is at times unbalanced, thank you for the food we have. There are many who are hungry.

Even though the routine of my job is often monotonous, thank you for the opportunity to work. There are many who have no job.

Even though I grumble and bemoan my fate from day to day and wish my circumstances were not so modest, thank you for life.

*Your body will love you
each time you recognize,
All the neat things that it does
like seeing "eye to eye."*

How to Say *Thank You* to Your Body

Acknowledgment. Recognition. Appreciation.

Do you say *thank you* to your body with positive acknowledgment, recognition and appreciation? Do you speak kindly about your body? Are you thankful for all you are able to do?

It is my belief that if we said *thank you* to our body as often as the pharmaceutical companies advertise drugs on television and in print, I think there would be less need for prescription medications.

There are many noteworthy people who also believe in the benefits of positive thoughts and words about the body. Louise Hay, Bernie Siegel and Norman Cousins have proven how well the body responds to acknowledgment, recognition and appreciation, particularly in overcoming challenging illnesses and disease.

Louise Hay, an international leader in inspirational and self-help publishing, discovered the power of acknowledging her body when she was diagnosed with cancer. She delayed having surgery to see if she could learn the source of the disease. What she found was that the cause of her cancer was based upon certain emotions and feelings about herself. When she developed and practiced a protocol of positive thoughts and affirmative words, she became cancer-free.

As a result of her healing, the road to prominence for

Louise Hay began when she hosted meetings in her home to teach the importance of self-acknowledgment. I attended a meeting about 25 years ago and learned the words to a song by Jai Josephs that I still sing today. I have found it to be an excellent way of saying *thank you* to myself. The words are:

I love myself the way I am
There's nothing that needs to change.
I'll always be, the perfect me
There's nothing to rearrange.

I'm beautiful, I'm capable
Of being the best me I can.
And I love myself
Just the way I am.

After singing the song several times, she had each person look into a hand mirror and say, "I love myself." The tears flowed as many of the participants including me had never done that previously.

An unknown writer offers this perspective about self-acknowledgment:

Society places different values on talents. A person who is talented in business or a specific profession is accorded a higher status than one whose talent is in sewing, cooking, repairing appliances, or hanging wallpaper. Yet, each talent is truly equal in value to every other talent.

The person who sews, knits or cooks with great skill is entitled to the same acknowledgment as the successful president of a major corporation. Each is entitled to be treated as a superstar. However, until we view what we do as important and valuable, no one else will. Others will view us as superstars when we give thanks and view ourselves that way.

Hmm…seeing ourselves as superstars and giving thanks? Do we? I think we are much better at acknowledging others than ourselves. I know that was true for me until I realized how unfair it was for me to ignore my feelings or my body.

How dare I expect my body to do everything I want, when I want and how I want, without saying *thank you*? My body does so much for me. In return, it deserves constant acknowledgment and appreciation from me. I hope this chapter encourages you to do the same.

One of the most startling discoveries I made about the value of self-acknowledgment is with injuries, trauma—hurts of any kind. I first wrote about this *thank you* idea in my *StarHeart Express* quarterly newsletter. Readers were quick to share their own experiences after first telling me how they thought I was crazy. This is what I suggested:

If you stub your toe, what is your first reaction? Anger? Embarrassment? Is it possible that you swear at your toe? Tell yourself how stupid?

Next question: How often have you noticed a bruise and had no idea how it got there? Did it ever cross your mind that if you acknowledged your body when you bumped any part of it, or slipped and fell, that your body might be satisfied without developing a bruise to get your attention?

What if I just stopped the minute I had an injury, no matter how small or seemingly insignificant, and really acknowledged that area of my body with love and a big *thank you*? Would the pain or bruise be less or not at all? Remembering the power of words, I decided to find out.

The first time I tried it was in the middle of the night when I got up and promptly walked into a door jam. All at once, I heard a crack and felt a good whack on my nose. Making it back to bed, I rubbed my hands together and put them over my nose. I apologized to my nose, acknowledged it for all that it does for me and thanked it profusely. When I woke up the next morning, there was no bruise, no soreness. Nothing!

On another occasion, I was in a beauty salon and a fluorescent ceiling light fell on my forearm smacking it pretty hard. People rushed over and there I was talking to my arm just like we do with little children. Again, no bruising. No soreness.

For me, the two experiences validate that the body truly responds to self-acknowledgment and appreciation. Since then I have had countless times to practice and to this day, it always works! Once in a while a bruise shows up telling me that I missed a chance to acknowledge and say *thank you* to my body.

If I were to pick out one part of my body to which I would write the biggest *thank you* note, it would have to be the liver. Do you know that the liver is responsible for over 500 functions in the body? Five hundred!

Do you know that if a processing plant were built to replicate all that the liver does, it would require a building one square block, five stories tall? That's why a compromised liver plays a role in nearly every disease of the human body. There are specific *thank you* ideas for the liver later in this chapter. First, here's a general suggestion for saying *thank you* to your body.

Think about a specific part of your body such as your knees, your legs, your heart or your big toe and say *thank you* as often as possible. To help you, here is a list from A to Z with an adjective for each letter of the alphabet to use with *thank you* rhymes or in little songs if you are so inclined.

Thank you…adorable arm, appendix and ankles.

Thank you…brilliant brain.

Thank you…clean colon.

Thank you…delightful digestive tract.

Thank you…exciting eyes and elbows.

Thank you…fantastic femur bones, feet and fingers.

Thank you…great gallbladder.

Thank you…happy heart, hips and hands.

Thank you…intelligent intestines.

Thank you…justly jaws.

Thank you…kind kidneys and knees.

Thank you…lovely lungs, liver and lips.

Thank you…magnificent muscles and mouth.

Thank you…nice nose.

Thank you…outrageous ovaries.

Thank you…precious pancreas and prostate.

Any ideas for the letter "Q?"

Thank you…rosy red blood cells.

Thank you…super spleen, sternum, shins and skin.

Thank you…terrific thyroid and toes.

Thank you…unique uterus.

Thank you…vivacious veins and vagina.

Thank you…wonderful white blood cells.

And… X, Y, Z… you tell me!

While I am waiting for your answer, here are more ways to say *thank you* to your body.

Breathing

I will let the experts do the talking about why conscious attention to your breathing is so important. This is what they have to say:

From Dr. Otto Warburg, president, Institute of Cell Physiology, Nobel Prize Winner:

"Deep breathing techniques which increase oxygen to the cells are the most important factors in living a disease free and energetic life. Remember, where cells get enough oxygen, cancer will not, cannot occur." Dr. Warburg is the only person to ever win the Nobel Prize for Medicine twice, and he was nominated for a third.

From Dr. Michael Yessis, Ph.D, President Sports Training Institute, Fitness Writer, *Muscle and Fitness Magazine:*

"Breathing correctly is the key to better fitness, muscle strength, stamina and athletic endurance."

From Dr. Sheldon Hendler, author of *The Oxygen Breakthrough MD Medical Researcher Cell Oxygenation:*

"Oxygenation through deep breathing boosts the immune system and can rid the body of chronic illnesses."

From Dr. J.W. Shields, Lymph, Lymph Glands, and Homeostasis, Lymphology:

"Deep diaphragmatic breathing stimulates the cleansing of the lymph system by creating a vacuum effect which pulls the lymph through the bloodstream. This increases the rate of toxic elimination by as much as 15 times the normal rate."

From Stephen Levine, a respected molecular biologist and geneticist, and Dr. Paris M. Kidd, Ph.D, Antioxidant Adaptation:

"Oxygen plays a pivotal role in the proper functioning of the immune system. We can look at oxygen deficiency as the single greatest cause of all diseases."

See the chapter Notes for a couple of breathing techniques to improve your energy and promote healing. A fantastic website that gives you verbal and visual cues for breathing is also listed. For now, say *thank you* to your body with a deep inhalation counting up to 20 and then exhale very slowly to the count of 20. Every time you stop and do just that much, you are saying a big *thank you*.

Eliminate Toxic Chemicals

Whether or not you believe that personal and household products are toxic for you, there are over 25,000 chemicals and substances that can potentially be used in shampoos, skin care items, perfumes, cleaning products, toothpastes, sun blocks and more. Anything we put on our skin, inhale while we are cleaning or use to wash ourselves or our clothes, it is a fact that the liver has to filter ALL substances.

Since the liver has to detoxify everything we ingest, put on our skin and inhale, it becomes overloaded with an excess of chemicals to filter. A stressed liver challenges the immune system which is the body's first line of defense against illness and disease.

From a top ten list of toxic chemicals that I have kept forever, you can do some research and decide for yourself which you want to avoid in products:

1. Alcohol, Isopropyl (SD-40)

2. DEA (diethanolamine), MEA (monoethanolamine), and TEA (triethanolamine)

3. DMDM Hydantoin

4. Urea (imidazolidinyl)

5. FD&C Color Pigments

6. Mineral Oil

7. Polyethylene glycol (PEG)

8. Propylene Glycol (PG) and Butylene Glycol

9. Sodium Lauryl Sulfate (SLS)

10. Triclosan—a common antibacterial ingredient

Gratefully, more companies are developing toxic-free products. For example, Miracle II offers a product line consisting of a lotion and two soaps that are chemical-free, and the first ingredient is prayer. There is a moisturizing soap for your body and regular strength soap for cleaning, laundry, dishwashing, windows and car washing.

For fragrances, essential oils make great perfumes. A combination of salt and soda is excellent for toothpaste and castor oil works well on hands and feet when they need a soothing balm.

I know your body will love you when you say *thank you* by reducing the use of toxic chemicals.

Feldenkrais

The Feldenkrais Method is an educational system intended to give greater functional awareness of the body. The method uses movement and mindfulness as the primary vehicle for learning.

I have found Feldenkrais tapes by Eileen Bach-y-Rita are very effective for reducing muscle discomfort from prolonged computer use and increasing my range of motion. If I can't finish a half-hour tape, even 10-15 minutes makes me feel like a new person. I can almost hear my body say *thank you*. Eileen's website is listed in the chapter Notes.

Gems of the Earth

Love is in the Earth is a reference book by Melody (no last name) describing the metaphysical properties and earth's energy stored in more than 1,000 minerals. I believe using the earth's minerals for healing and other benefits is an elegant way to say *thank you* to the body. I have listed some of my favorite gemstones along with a brief description about their purpose.

Amber—allows the body to heal itself by absorbing and transmuting negative energy into positive energy. It emits a sunny and bright soothing energy which helps to calm nerves and enliven disposition. Amber cleanses the environment in which it rests.

Carnelian—stimulates analytical capabilities, precision and it protects against envy, fear, rage and other negativity. Carnelian is useful for increasing physical energy, personal power, creativity and compassion.

Hematite—called the "stone for the mind," hematite helps one to sort things out. It can be used for mental attunement, memory enhancement, original thinking and technical knowledge. Hematite also helps to facilitate peace, self-control and inner happiness.

Jasper—known as the "supreme nurturer" it protects against negativity and helps one to be grounded. This mineral balances the yin-yang energy and the physical, emotional and intellectual bodies. This is a real gem for soothing the nerves.

Labradorite—assists with changes, attracts strength and perseverance. It enhances patience and an inner knowing of the right time.

Lapis—energizes the throat chakra, it is the "stone of total awareness." It helps maintain objectivity, assists with dreams and is used for the treatment of disorders of the throat, bone marrow, thymus and immune system.

Pearl—signifies faith, clarity, and innocence, enhances personal integrity and helps provide focus. It's known as the stone of sincerity.

Quartz—amplifies both energy and thoughts. There are numerous kinds of quartz crystals such as rose, citrine, amethyst and so many more.

Vanadinite—promotes order and helps define goals and the pursuit of goals in an orderly manner.

Gluten Free

Studies show that inflammation is a major source of pain and malfunction because the body just can't do its job with inflamed tissues. If inflammation can be reduced or eliminated, your body will say *thank you* with better health and well-being.

Gluten has been identified as a source of inflammation in the body. It is a special type of protein that is commonly found in wheat, rye and barley. Since most baked goods, cereals and breads contain one or more of these three grains, the potential is high for excessive consumption of gluten.

There are grains that are gluten-free including wild rice, corn, buckwheat, millet, amaranth, quinoa, teff, oats, soybeans and spelt. Using more of these grains in your diet reduces or possibly eliminates inflammation caused by eating foods containing gluten.

One of my favorite substitutes for gluten-free grains is quinoa, first discovered in South America over 5,000 years ago. There are quinoa flakes for a quick hot cereal, grains like rice for cooking and quinoa flour used for breads and pastas. Quinoa is a balanced source of protein that is easy to digest and is higher in amino acids than other grains. Make an adventure out of finding gluten-free alternatives and recipes for cookies, muffins or breads.

Go Green

It has been reported that the standard, high-carbohydrate, low-protein diet disrupts the body's ability to adequately regulate blood sugar, forcing it to produce too much insulin. By contrast, foods low on the glycemic index chart calm the body and reduce the potential for inflammation.

A dietary choice that says *thank you* to your body is to "think green" when it comes to food. The liver thrives on anything green except for mold. A partial list is: beet greens, broccoli, chard, green beans and peas (black-eyed peas don't count), kale, lettuce, mustard greens, sprouts (alfalfa, sunflower), spinach and zucchini to name a few.

Green vegetables are important for the liver because

they cleanse and regenerate it plus they provide natural vitamins and minerals. They are slow digesting carbohydrates that help you stay calm and centered. Using green "veggies" in place of stimulating foods (corn, wheat, dairy, soybeans and fruit), help you think clearly, work more efficiently and definitely sleep better.

Herbs such as basil, cilantro, oregano, rosemary, sage and thyme are great seasonings for green vegetables. Do you know that sage is the herb of thanksgiving? *Thank you*, Shirley, for that little tidbit!

All in all, eating herbs and green vegetables is a fantastic way to say *thank you* to your body—especially the liver!

H2O = Water

Blood is 83 percent water, muscles are 75 percent water, the brain is 74 percent water and bone is 22 percent water. Nutritionists claim that up to 80 percent of the U.S. population is dehydrated. Coffee, tea and sodas containing caffeine not only don't make a good substitute for water, they cause the body to lose water.

The liver and kidneys require water to detoxify and carry away wastes from the body. If you want vitamins and nutrients absorbed, think water. When it comes to digestion, fiber alone cannot aid proper digestive function. In fact, without drinking plenty of water between meals (not during the meal), good fiber goes bad causing constipation and other discomfort.

The blood thickens when the body is dehydrated making circulation more difficult. This condition causes the brain to be sluggish, challenges concentration and the end result is fatigue. All because of a lack of water!

Say *thank you* to your body by drinking half your weight as the number of ounces you drink each day. Make it fun—decorate a water glass or line up the equivalent amount of filled water bottles to help you keep track.

Now, if you will excuse me while I get a drink of water. *Thank you!*

Laughter

Children know intuitively that laughter is the best. They laugh hundreds of times a day while adults are known to laugh 10-15 times by comparison.

Norman Cousins was one of the leaders in proving laughter is the best medicine when he wrote about his own healing in the book, *Anatomy of an Illness.*

Dr. Madan Kataria, a medical doctor from India, studied the Norman Cousins story. Along with other research, he was motivated to develop Laughter Yoga that is practiced in more 7,000 laughter clubs throughout the world. There are no jokes; nothing to make fun of. People simply laugh for exercise.

From his book, *Laugh for No Reason*, Dr. Kataria states: "Laughter makes us feel good because it diffuses three of the most painful emotions (fear, anger and boredom) by releasing them. That release prevents or stops conflicts, eases tension and helps people to better see others' point of view.

"Laughter Yoga aims to develop joyfulness, not happiness. In contrast to happiness, joyfulness is the unconditional commitment to having fun despite all the problems that we are faced with in life. Joyfulness is primarily a physical phenomenon. You fake it until you get it.

"The decision may come from the brain but the process is physical because the body and the mind are so closely interconnected when you 'do good' or you 'feel good.' Motion creates emotion. Being joyful and doing good changes the body chemistry and fosters a healthier state of being.

"Laughter changes frustration to fascination, frees us from inhibitions, and wakes up the child in us. You don't have to have a sense of humor to practice laughter yoga."

Laughter Yoga has been featured on *Oprah*, *Dancing with the Stars*, *Geraldo Rivera*, *Good Morning America* and *CNN* to name a few. Websites for information about laughter clubs, leader training and more are listed in the chapter Notes. There are also suggestions for how to laugh on your own. *Thank you*, Jeffrey, for starting the Laguna Beach Laughter Club.

Massage

Bodywork is powerful. Regardless of the adjectives assigned to it (pampering, rejuvenating, therapeutic) or the reasons we enjoy it (a luxurious treat, stress relief, pain management), massage therapy is an ally in your healthcare regimen—a magnificent way to say *thank you* to your body.

Experts estimate that close to 90 percent of all disease is stress related. Massage techniques reduce stress because they activate more oxygen into the tissues. Reducing stress translates into decreased anxiety, enhanced sleep quality, greater energy, improved concentration, increased circulation and less fatigue.

There are many types of massage—aromatherapy, back, deep tissue, hot stone, pregnancy, reflexology, shiatsu, sports, Swedish and watsu which is done in a warm-water pool. I love saying *thank you* to my body with Ortho-Bionomy®, a muscle-adjustment type of massage. It is a gentle, non-invasive form of body therapy, highly effective in working with chronic stress, injuries and pains, or problems associated with postural and structural imbalances. *Thank you*, Rouel. You are a great practitioner of this work.

Meditation

Meditation is scientifically proven to reduce stress, blood pressure, heart disease and anxiety. Practiced regularly, meditation also increases mental abilities, focus, concentration, longevity and creates the consciousness to be in control of your life. In her book, *Daily Guidance from Your*

Angels, Doreen Virtue has this description of meditation: "Your free and portable agent whose only side effects are peace of mind and rejuvenation."

As I mentioned in the introduction, the words *thank you* are my mantra, my meditation. Whether I am sitting in a quiet, peaceful pose or traveling down the freeway in my car, I use the words *thank you* to center my attention. This practice helps me feel gratitude in my mind, body and spirit.

There are many websites offering information about the benefits of meditation as well as products to help you with your practice. One in particular is hosted by Gary van Warmerdam. When I found his website, I was thrilled to meet a kindred spirit who shares my belief about the importance of saying *thank you* to the body. His website features a *thank you* meditation and with his permission, I am including it here. *Thank you,* Gary.

Thank You Life

Thank you for this breath
Thank you for this inhale
Thank you for this exhale
Thank you for this Life

Thank you Heart
Thank you for this pounding
Thank you for this pulsing
Thank you for this Love

Thank you feet
Thank you for this walk
Thank you for this run
Thank you for the Dancing

Thank you Eyes
Thank you for the Sunrise
Thank you for the Sunset
Thank you for all the Colors

Thank you Ears
Thank you for The Music
Thank you for the Rhythm
And Thank you for the Stillness

Thank you Hands
Thank you for the Caressing
Thank you for the Clapping
And Thank you for the Holding

Thank you Mouth
Thank you for the nourishment
Thank you for the Wine
Thank you for the Kisses

Thank you Nose
Thank you for the Flowers
Thank you for the Pines
Thank you for the Sniffles

Thank you Arms and Shoulders
Thank you for the Carrying
Thank you for the Burdening
And Thank you for the Hugging

Thank you Voice
Thank you for the Expression
Thank you for the Word
Thank you for the Gift of Creation

Thank you for this Day
Thank you for the Light
Thank you for the Stars
Thank you for the Night

Thank you Self
Thank you for the Laughter
Thank you for the Play
Thank you for You

Thank you for the Emotions
Thank you for the Joys
Thank you for the Tears and Sorrows
Thank you for the Richness

Thank you for the Abundance that is.
Thank you for the Abundance that is given.
Thank you for the so many experiences and so many things
Thank you for this Dance.

Thank you Life

Pain Free PC

Anyone spending more than an hour a day at the computer needs to say a special *thank you* by getting up every 30 minutes, stretching, drinking water and doing a few simple exercises. This is an absolute must for the body to know you acknowledge, recognize and appreciate all it does for you as you sit and send emails, surf the net and perform many other tasks.

In the book, *Pain Free at Your PC*, Pete Egoscue talks about drinking plenty of water while using the computer to reduce pain, soreness and inflammation. Think about a manufacturing plant and how water is used to keep the mechanics from getting too hot. When it comes to using the computer, the same is true of our bodies, particularly the fingers, hands, wrists, arms, elbows and shoulders.

For extended computer use, Egoscue has a five-minute routine on pages 114-121 that is extremely beneficial. While I was writing THANKYOUOLOGY, each time the clock chimed on the hour, I went to another chair and did the recommended five exercises in five minutes. I call it my "five for five" routine. *Thank you, Pete!*

Skin Brushing

The skin is the largest organ in the body. On a daily basis, it is responsible for one-fourth of the body's detoxification, making it one of the most important organs for elimination.

Skin brushing has so many benefits. It tightens the skin, helps digestion, removes cellulite, stimulates circulation and cleans the lymphatic system. Skin brushing also removes dead skin layers, strengthens the immune system, improves the exchange between cells and stimulates the glands, helping all of the body systems to perform at peak efficiency.

The simple skin brushing steps are described in the chapter Notes. It is worth your time to add skin brushing to your morning routine before taking a shower—a most invigorating way to say *thank you* to your body.

Take Time

Time. How are you spending yours? I have always said that we don't need stress management training if we stop trying to mix water and oil. That's my way of saying that we can keep from overloading our time if we pay attention to what we do with it.

Using a month-at-a-glance calendar makes it easy to see when days or evenings are filling up. When my schedule starts to fill up, I mark off the next day or evening to:

Take the time to think…it is the source of power.

Take the time to play…it is the secret of keeping young.

Take the time to read…it is the source of knowledge.

Take the time to pray…it is the greatest power on earth.

Take the time to make friends…it is the road to happiness.

Take the time to laugh…it is the music of the soul.

Take the time to give…it is the price of success.

Take the time to be charitable…it is the key to Heaven.

Take the time to love…it is the grace of God.

Walking

Following in my mom's footsteps, walking first thing in the morning has been a lifelong habit. Even in my travels, I am always up and out the door walking on a beach, by a stream, down a path, along a road or around the neighborhood. I have to walk! This habit has kept me mentally and physically in shape, also I have many stories about the people I meet and the sights I see.

The research on the benefits of walking is extensive. I believe some of the more prominent reasons to walk are for maintaining or reducing weight, lowering blood pressure, strengthening the heart and for better bone health to prevent broken hips and other signs of osteoporosis.

In addition to the health and well-being benefits of walking, there are so many things you can do while walking—take the time to observe your surroundings, listen to the birds, watch the changing lighting of the sky, notice your breath, feel your body feeling happy, swing your arms, sing a song and oh yes, make up *thank you* rhymes!

Some people drink coffee to wake up and get going; I prefer my walks and I know my body does too.

———

Oh my, this action-oriented list for saying *thank you* to the body is just a sample of the discoveries I have enjoyed since I recognized the importance of self-acknowledgment. And, I already hear myself asking: *What about stretching or self-hugs?* I will let you add those and others to your list as you develop your own practice of saying *thank you* to your body.

Why is it so important to say *thank you* to the body? Without your health, does anything else matter? There was a time in my life when aches and pain, allergies, injuries and emotional/mental stress were common. Before I was thirty years old, I had five surgeries—two were on my back!

Reflecting on the early years of my life, I would say that I was functioning mostly from the neck up, which is my way of saying that I didn't really have a mind-body-spirit connection. When I faced the fact that I couldn't trade my body in for a new and improved model, I knew it was imperative to take care of the one I had.

Deciding that surgery and prescription drugs did not give me the level of health I believed possible, I made a conscious choice to see what alternatives were available to support my well-being. When I connected with the idea of saying *thank you* to my body, I loved having 24/7 access to a tool that empowered me to take charge of my healing and health. With *thank you* recognition and appreciation for my body, I found it much more enjoyable to "live in it." I lost interest in wanting to "trade it in" and gained momentum in helping my body to "be all it could be."

The process of saying *thank you* to my body has been similar to peeling an onion—the more I give my body acknowledgment and appreciation, the more I enjoy health and well-being. With that foundation, if I have a physical challenge, I facilitate my healing with *thank you* tools such as laughter, meditation, walking or taking time out. I use *thank you* rhymes and affirmations to keep my thoughts and words focused on wellness.

If I need outside intervention, I use *thank you* affirmations to attract what or who I need. For example, when I said *thank you* for a spiritual nutritionist, my friend Tina had an excellent referral for me. The practitioner suggested a dietary plan that made total sense to me: raw nuts and seeds, green vegetables, raw oils such as sesame and olive, and protein with every meal. Dairy, corn, soybean, sugar and wheat are "out" and eating every two to three hours is "in." My energy stays up and internal/external stress is down. For me, it's a winning combination. *Thank you*, Shannon!

What I love most about saying *thank you* to my body is

how connected I feel to it as a result. Because I feel such a connection to ME, I feel so much awareness of what works for me and what does not. I find that I have the strength to say "no" when I need to and "yes" when I want to.

This understanding of myself and what works best prompted the idea of writing my own operating instructions. Every manufactured item I know of has directions for how to use and operate the product. Since we are not born with these "directions" in hand, I believe it is a good idea to figure them out and honor them. With this awareness, you are also able to guide others concerning what works for you and what doesn't. My *Operating Instructions* are included in the chapter Notes as an example for you to create your own.

Ultimately, having a healthy mind-body-spirit connection with the art of saying *thank you* boosts your self-worth, self-assurance and self-confidence. It is with a strong sense of self that you live an empowered life—a life where you thrive physically, mentally, emotionally and spiritually. In order to see "eye to eye" on this THANKYOUOLOGY principle, remember the following:

You are the only one there is
you are brilliance indeed,
Recognize your body with thank you
and receive everything you need.

You have the power
to take charge of your health,
With thank you thoughts and words
they are worth abundant wealth!

Notes
....

Activities

1. Compose a list of ways you would like to say *thank you* to your body. Post it where you can see it or put it in the front of your journal book. Review your list each day making check marks next to those that you practiced. Note improvements and write *thank you* when you do.

2. Make a copy of the A to Z adjectives to help you with the habit of saying *thank you* to every part of your body. Practice this regularly and see a big difference in your health and well-being.

3. Create simple poems to remind you of how special everything is in your body. Here are two examples:

   Thank You Adorable Arm
   It starts at the elbow
   and ends at the wrist,
   The arm is quite useful
   without it my hand would not exist.

   Thank You Beautiful Brain
   More than a computer
   smarter than anything under the sun,
   My brain is a worldly wonder
   I love using it and having lots of fun!

4. If an organized group is not nearby, laugh on your own! Here are some suggestions to get you started:

   • Look into a mirror and make funny faces.

   • Line up your palms and fingers, clap your hands in a cha-cha beat and say: ho-ho-ha-ha-ha!

   • Lie on the floor on your back and just start laughing. This is a super way to exercise the spine at the same time. Wave your hands, kick your feet, just let loose and have a good time!

- Take simple songs such as *Row, Row, Row Your Boat* and substitute HO-HO and HA-HA for the words. Singing a childhood song in such a silly way can have you laughing in no time.

- Greet your plants, furniture, anything around you with laughter. Bet it makes their day!

- Think about how you are doing these things to laugh for exercise and the mere thought should really make you laugh!

At the Workplace

If your company has an employee newsletter, submit an article sharing share your favorite way of saying *thank you* to your body. Offer to make it a regular column to help others recognize the importance of practicing this form of saying *thank you*.

Do some additional research about the health benefits of laughter yoga and ask to have a laughter program at your workplace. It can be done for 10-15 minutes on breaks, at lunch (preferably before you eat), or after work.

References & Resources

Books

Norman Cousins
   Anatomy of an Illness

Pete Egoscue
   Pain Free at Your PC

Louise Hay
   Heal the Body

Dr. Madan Kataria
   Laugh For No Reason

Melody
  Love is in the Earth—A Kaleidoscope of Crystals

Doreen Virtue
  Daily Guidance from Your Angels

Directions for Skin Brushing

1. Buy a natural, not synthetic bristle brush to avoid scratching the skin. Remember this is about saying *thank you*.

2. Make sure it has a long handle so you can reach all areas of your body.

3. Skin brush before showering at least once a day… twice a day is even better!

4. Make sure the skin is dry.

5. Start with the soles of the feet first, next the ankles, calves, thighs, stomach, hands and arms.

6. Do circular, counter-clockwise strokes on the abdomen. Lighter strokes around the breasts and no brushing the nipples.

7. Vigorously brush the entire body several times.

8. While brushing, this is another opportunity to say *thank you* to every area of the body. How cool is that?

9. Take a warm shower followed by a cool rinse to invigorate and stimulate.

10. Wash the brush every few weeks in warm soapy water and let dry.

My Operating Instructions

What I love most is time
time is the source of my power,
Let me rise and shine at leisure
that works better than a particular hour.

I work best when I observe
and think about the meanings,
Of what I see and what I hear
sometimes it goes through many screenings.

Make sure I have the time to play
I love spur of the moments too,
When I am learning anything
it's better if it's done in fun with you.

Ah yes, please allow me time for reading
stories are my favorite indeed,
Especially those about people making a difference
by helping others who are in need.

Somewhere in the morning wake up time
it is definitely a good rule,
For me to be in silent prayer
that is my number one helpful tool.

There must be quality time with others
whether it is family, co-workers or a friend,
I thrive in sharing "food for thought"
I love to hear how ideas blend.

Laughter is a necessity
I giggle and wiggle with the best,
When I do my energy is high
and I am filled with humorous zest.

If you want to know what really
makes me tick above and beyond,
It's when I share my creative gifts
and wave my magic wand.

And, remember my favorite phrases
"quality over quantity" is at the top,
I believe in Seeing The Other Possibilities
that is my acronym for the word, STOP.

Speaking of words, I have many favorites
including grand, elegance and galore,
There's magnificence, magical and majestic
and by the way, I love being adored!

One final note about the way I think
I believe it is true and right,
That everyone is absolutely connected
to unlimited Love and Light.

These are my "operating instructions"
guided by grace from above,
I am grateful for all that I feel
I say thank you the most for Love.

Websites

Breathing
www.doasone.com

Feldenkrais
www.feldenkraisathome.com

Laughter Yoga
www.laughteryoga.org
www.LYinstitute.org
www.laughangeles.com

Meditation Guidance
www.centerpointe.com
www.meditationandmore.com
www.meditationsforwomen.com

Miracle II Products
www.miracleii.com

Ortho-Bionomy®
www.ortho-bionomy.org

Gary van Warmerdam
www.pathwaystohappiness.com

Yoga Breathing Techniques

The basic premise of Yoga Breathing is that the exhalation should be longer than the inhalation which will help to fill up the lungs with more air and increase their capacity.

1. Sit comfortably with your spine erect. Take a few deep breaths, relax and allow a free flow of breath. Inhale and let your belly expand. Exhale forcefully through the nostrils by contracting the abdominal muscles and then passively allow the inhalation to happen.

    Repeat this routine slowly up to 5 times. When this is comfortable, increase up to 20. Gradually pick up the pace to find your own rhythm.

    After each round, exhale completely holding the breath out briefly. Inhale briefly when needed while holding the breath. Exhale when ready and repeat or return to normal respiration.

2. Sit in a comfortable meditative pose keeping the spine erect and balanced. Left hand is kept on the left knee and the right hand is on the bridge of the nose with the fourth and the middle fingers on the left side of the nose. Only press on the bony region to control breathing.

    With the thumb, close off the right nostril and exhale through the left nostril. Then, inhale through that same nostril. Release the right nostril and press on the left nostril with the fourth and middle fingers while exhaling through the right nostril. Inhale through that same nostril and place the thumb back on the right nostril. Release the left nostril and exhale. Repeat slowly.

Thank You Quotes

Henry Ward Beecher: *Gratitude is the fairest blossom which springs from the soul.*

French Proverb: *Gratitude is the heart's memory.*

There are all those little things
that lots of people do,
How often do you take the time
to say how much it means to you?

How to Say *Thank You* to Others

Appreciation. Gratitude. Thankfulness.

After conducting a study of 1500 employees in scores of work settings, Dr. Gerald H. Graham, professor of management at Wichita State University, found that the most powerful motivator was personalized, instant recognition from their managers.

In the book, *1001 Ways to Reward Employees*, Bob Nelson cites from this same survey: "Only 42 percent of the respondents believed their managers personally congratulated employees who do a good job."

How is that possible? It costs nothing to say *thank you*. In fact, according to a study by the American Productivity Center in Houston and the American Compensation Association, it was found that it costs four percent of an employee's salary to give non-cash rewards while it takes five to eight percent if it is a cash reward.

There is also a flip side. The late Ann Landers featured a letter in her column written by a business owner. He said that after giving annual bonuses for 16 years, he was ending the practice because not one employee took the time to say *thank you*. How sad for all—the business owner who was not acknowledged by his employees and the employees who didn't think to express their appreciation.

From Don Martin's *Speakers on File*, there is a story

about a play that Fran Tarkenton, a well-known football player, made in a game where his team was behind in the score. He called a play requiring him to throw a block—a risky move for a quarterback because of the potential for injury. That play won the game for his team, the Minnesota Vikings.

The next day the coach was going over the details of the game with the players. After the meeting, Tarkenton went up to the coach and asked why he didn't say anything about the block. The coach told him that he always worked hard so he figured he didn't have to say anything. According to the story, the quarterback's response was, "If you ever want me to block again you do."

A little boy expressed that same message when he told his father: "Let's play darts. I'll throw and you say wonderful."

Do you want to be thanked? Acknowledged? Appreciated? Recognized? Then, GIVE what you love to receive. Applying the law of attraction to the art of saying *thank you*, the more you say *thank you* to others, the more others will acknowledge and appreciate you.

Saying *thank you* to others means recognizing opportunities to express meaningful appreciation and offering it regularly. In addition to saying the words, *thank you*, acknowledge people with your actions—a smile, a listening ear, a shoulder to lean on, an unexpected gesture of kindness—the list is endless. The more you say *thank you* to every person and situation in your life, the more you receive, as the following story demonstrates about a young man's winnings on the *Wheel of Fortune* game show.

Normally, contestants talk about jobs, family and hobbies. Before he said anything about himself, the contestant thanked the police officer who pulled him over for speeding while he was driving to the studio. When he told the officer that he was going to be a contestant on *Wheel of Fortune*, the officer did not give him a ticket so he could get to the studio on time.

The young man won over $60,000 in cash and prizes qualifying him to return on the Friday show as one of the top three winners—a previous format of the show. On that episode, he won an additional $50,000 in cash and prizes. His total winnings were $110,000—the highest amount any contestant had won in that season.

Do you think there was any connection with his *attitude of gratitude* at the beginning of the show and his subsequent winnings? I believe so!

I love reading about sports professionals who have made a dream come true with hard work and dedication. Hearing them thank those that helped them get where they are today is especially heartwarming.

Nomar Garciaparra, a baseball player for the Los Angeles Dodgers, thanked the fans and told them how much he appreciated them when he was interviewed for an article in the *Los Angeles Times*. He told how he remembered sitting in the bleachers as a kid and knew how lucky he was to be wearing the uniform of the team he had always idolized.

If you are a tennis fan, who could forget Andre Agassi's farewell speech at the U.S. Open in September 2006? He expressed appreciation and acknowledgment of the fans with these words: "You have given me your shoulders to stand on to reach my dreams, dreams I could not have reached without you."

Opportunities for acknowledging others may not seem obvious at first; the next two stories show how there is always more potential with conscious awareness.

Charles Plumb was a U.S. Navy pilot in Vietnam. After 75 combat missions, his plane was destroyed by a surface-to-air missile. Plumb ejected and parachuted into enemy hands. He was captured and spent six years in a communist Vietnamese prison. He survived the ordeal and now lectures on lessons learned from that experience.

One day when Plumb and his wife were sitting in a restaurant, a man at another table approached and called him by name. He also knew that Plumb flew jet fighters in Vietnam from the aircraft carrier Kitty Hawk and was shot down.

Plumb asked the gentleman how he knew. The man said that he packed his parachute and was glad to see it had worked. Plumb was surprised and expressed his gratitude as they shook hands.

That night Plumb couldn't sleep. He was thinking about the man who packed his parachute, the man he couldn't remember seeing on the Kitty Hawk. Finally he remembered. During his time on the aircraft carrier, his attitude was that he was a pilot and the others were just sailors.

Now when Plumb is speaking to his audiences, he motivates people to think about who is packing their parachute. He inspires folks to see every person as someone who has the potential to make a difference in their life.

A nursing student tells the story about a professor who gave a pop quiz. She breezed through the questions until she read the last one that asked: What is the first name of the woman who cleans the school? She thought the question was a joke.

She had seen the cleaning woman several times. She was tall, dark-haired and in her fifties. How was she to know her name? She handed in her paper leaving the last question blank. Before class ended, one student asked if the last question counted toward the quiz grade.

The professor told the class the last question on the quiz did matter. He reminded them how they would meet many people in their careers and each person would be significant. It was his belief that everyone deserves to be acknowledged even if it's with a smile and a quick hello.

The nurse never forgot that lesson about acknowledging others. She also learned the cleaning woman's name was Dorothy.

A teacher wanted to teach her students the importance of paying attention to others. She asked them to write down the name of each person in the class, and to say something nice about them. She collected the papers, compiled a page of comments from the classmates, and gave each student his or her own list.

Years later when she attended the funeral of one of the students, his father handed her a well-worn piece of paper. It was the list of all the nice things his classmates had said about him. He wasn't the only person to save his list. Other students came forward and shared how they had kept theirs as well. Proves that gold stars are hard to throw away!

What about when an opportunity to express appreciation is overlooked or missed? Chris Peterson, a psychology professor at the University of Michigan gave his students an assignment to write a "belated gratitude" letter. Studies show that the writer often gets more of a boost than the receiver. It has also been found that the benefits are even greater if the letter is read to the recipient in person. According to positive psychology experts, the gratitude visit is the most effective aspect of this activity.

I think teachers and professors are definitely worthy candidates for what I call "belated *thank you*" letters. I love stories about those who finally receive the praise they deserve.

Jim Hosney, a retiring teacher at Crossroads School for Arts and Sciences in Santa Monica, California was surprised when he was honored by Hollywood's "who's who" along with many of his students whose lives he touched for more than 25 years of teaching. According to a *Los Angeles Times* article about the event, some of the most prominent people in show business attribute their value as artists to him.

A letter appeared in an Ann Landers column from a woman who wrote that she had become a successful artist. When she learned her art teacher was going to be attending her fiftieth class reunion, the artist wrote the teacher a letter of appreciation. The evening of the event, the teacher told her that in all her years of teaching, she was the first of her students to write and say, *thank you*.

A professor at CSU Fullerton regularly told his students that when they became successful because of the business principles he taught, they could say *thank you* with a Porsche. Imagine the professor's surprise when many years later one of his students called to ask him what color and delivered a maroon Porsche Boxster the following day!

Instead of paying it forward, I call belated expressions of gratitude "paying it backward." I say it's time to get out that yearbook, find those favorite teachers and let them know how their efforts have helped you in life. You may also acknowledge a special teacher through Donors Choose, a non-profit organization that accepts donations for specific school needs that teachers identify on the agency's website.

It's obvious from these inspiring stories and many more like them that saying *thank you* to others reaps big benefits both for the person saying it, as well as the one receiving words of appreciation and recognition.

To practice saying *thank you* to others more often, start with the most important folks in your life—your family. Here is a list of questions (think of it as a pop quiz) to help you see opportunities to say *thank you*. I know you will think of more.

Who takes out the trash? Mows the lawn? Who makes breakfast? Packs the lunches? Prepares dinner? How about cleaning the house? Doing the laundry? Running errands? Is there a new project that someone is in charge of? What about accomplishments such as good grades? Making a sports or dance team? Who makes you laugh? Who is there for you when you are feeling down? What about the person who keeps cheering you on? Each time you say *thank you* to your loved ones, you are creating positive energy that gives back to you as well.

What about your extended family of aunts, uncles, grandfathers, grandmothers and cousins? Have they been thanked for their cards and gifts acknowledging your birthday, graduation, wedding or other gift-giving occasions? What about kind gestures that are often overlooked such as being a good listener, offering words of encouragement or assisting you with your education or career? Write those *thank you* letters and express your appreciation. They deserve to be acknowledged even if it's an overdue *thank you*.

Next, ask yourself how often you say *thank you* to your friends for all the kindnesses they do for you. Do they loan you things, help you with ideas or offer assistance in some way? Have they watched your children? Are they a good listening ear? Is their perspective valuable to you? Have you taken the time to tell them how you feel about the neat things that they do for you?

Saying *thank you* is extremely valuable in your professional life since there is no "I" in the word team. Recognize co-workers and the role each plays in the success of your job. Acknowledge them through emails, in person or give them a surprise call to say, *thank you*.

Thoughts and words of appreciation for others is augmented with gratitude actions. Following are action-oriented *thank you* suggestions:

A Family *Thank You* Campaign

Use colorful paper or sticky notes to write *thank you* notes to everyone in your household. Hide them like Easter eggs—in lunch boxes for the kids (do they still make lunch boxes?), in shoes, on the computer, at the door, in a briefcase. Make it fun, do it often and enjoy what happens!

Thank You at Celebration Dinners

Before a holiday meal begins, take time to acknowledge friends and family. When everyone is seated at the table, light a candle and have one person start with a *thank you* to the person on the left or right. When that person is finished, the candle is passed to the next person who repeats the gesture until everyone has given and received an acknowledgment. A great way to start the meal!

Thank You with Recycled Greeting Cards

Instead of tossing out your holiday greeting cards, keep them in a box or bag. Throughout the year, regularly select one to reread. Then write a *thank you* note to the sender telling that person something you appreciate about your friendship or business relationship.

Thank You Thoughts

Having a tough time with a particular person? Had a falling out or lost contact with others all together? Write each name on a piece of paper, fold it and put all of them in an envelope. After your morning journal writing, select one of the folded names and say *thank you* to that person. Every time you think about the person during the day, say *thank you* to help shift your feelings about the person. Record your results in your journal and repeat as often as necessary.

Thank You to Those Who Pack Your Parachute

During the holidays, people typically remember to say *thank you* to those who provide services throughout the year. How about making it a regular practice by setting up a reminder program on your computer, cell phone or blackberry? If you still pay a bill with a check and return envelope, write a *thank you* note on the enclosed stub or make it a point to express your appreciation in person.

Some of the people that deserve a *thank you* note include your auto mechanic, baker, banker, beautician, computer technician, dentist, doctor, dog/cat groomer, dry cleaners, fitness trainer, grocer, insurance agent, jeweler, landscape/gardener, manicurist, optometrist, pest maintenance person, pharmacist, plumber, printer, restaurateur, teacher, tailor, travel agent and veterinarian.

Acknowledging Famous Folks

In a *Dear Abby* column, I loved the letter from a 13-year-old boy expressing his gratitude to an inspirational speaker at his school who helped him understand the price of freedom. What public figure has inspired you or done something that you could acknowledge with a note of appreciation? City leaders? Columnists? Television or radio broadcasters? Fire or police department personnel? Hospital volunteers? Lifeguards? Librarians? Nurses?

When celebrities do something you admire, send them a *thank you* note expressing your appreciation. I think it's great that Montel Williams is using his celebrity status to be a voice for people with multiple sclerosis while Michael J. Fox is doing the same on behalf of Parkinson's disease. I would like to say *thank you* to both of these gentlemen for being an inspiration to others who have the same health challenges.

Saying *Thank You* in a Big Way

If you have an extraordinary situation in your city, county, state or want to acknowledge something worldwide, with the help of the internet and other accessible communication tools, start a campaign just like Shauna Fleming did with the *A Million Thanks* program. Her mission was to send one million letters of appreciation to the troops serving overseas. More than four million people responded with their thanks to the men and women in military roles.

Morrill Worcester also likes to say *thank you* in a big way. For the past 14 years, he has provided a wreath for each grave at Arlington National Cemetery in Virginia. Every year a truck rolls up in the early morning hours and volunteers help him place the wreaths. Because of an email wave in 2007, hundreds of volunteers joined him that year in saying *thank you* to the men and women who have died protecting the freedoms of our country.

As a former television news director, I am grateful to the media for covering these heartwarming efforts that all started with one person's desire to say, *thank you*.

Thank You Notes in the Workplace

The customer service programs of such companies as Hallmark and Southwest Airlines are often used as models of success for other businesses and corporations. They have fine-tuned the art of saying *thank you* to their customers and spend a lot of money doing it.

If you are self-employed, acknowledging customers doesn't have to be expensive or time consuming. Speaking from the heart is what matters. In the chapter Notes, there are examples of poetic *thank you* notes for customers of CPA's, hair stylists, real estate agents and entrepreneurs that have a staff.

I believe job applicants should also be thought of as customers and treated as such. You never know the potential relationship of an applicant regardless of whether they are hired or not. It takes just a minute to reply to an online application with the words, *thank you*, or to send a post card acknowledging receipt of an application in the mail. Because of how I was treated during the application and an interview process, I am a regular donor to a non-profit organization even though I did not receive an employment offer.

Saying *Thank You* to Mother Nature

Acknowledging Mother Nature with a grateful heart is a powerful daily meditation. Take a walk in your backyard, around the block or in a nearby park. Notice everything—the grass, the trees, the plants, the flowers. Observe the abundance of leaves. Feel the breeze and the sunlight. Count the raindrops when they are falling. Soak up the vastness of it all. And, remember to say *thank you* with each step!

———

I couldn't finish this chapter on the art of saying *thank you* to others without including a story about one of my heroes, Walt Disney.

As a native of Southern California, I grew up going to Disneyland and watching Disney movies. While I wasn't at the Magic Kingdom on opening day, I was at Disneyland 50 years later celebrating the kick-off of the anniversary party that lasted 18 months for the "happiest place on earth."

I believe Walt Disney was a master at saying *thank you* based on the book, *How to Be Like Walt*, written by Pat Williams with Jim Denney. This book is a superb resource for any business that wants to increase its customer service performance. What I call the art of saying *thank you*, Walt Disney called "plussing."

"Plussing" was Walt's way of keeping customers. He believed that if a customer stopped visiting the park, it would cost ten times more to get them back. That is why he constantly added attractions and events for the guests. It was his way of saying, *thank you*.

Of all the stories in the book, my favorite is about the family who was visiting Disney World for the first time. When asked what the highlight of their vacation was, their response was that they liked going back to the hotel at night. They were excited to see how the maid arranged the child's dolls each day. According to the book, the dolls were "perched on the edge of the bathtub, hanging from a light fixture or sitting inside a boat made out of the towels." Can you imagine the look on their faces when they returned to a room so magically detailed? What a way to say, *thank you*!

And the last *"thank you* to others" story is a most precious one indeed.

In the days when an ice cream sundae cost much less, a 10-year-old boy entered a hotel coffee shop and sat at a table.

When a waitress put a glass of water in front of him and he asked, "How much is an ice cream sundae?"

"Fifty cents," she replied.

The little boy pulled his hand out of his pocket and studied the number of coins in it. "How much is a dish of plain ice cream?" he inquired. Some people were now waiting for a table and the waitress was a bit impatient.

"Thirty-five cents," she said brusquely.

The little boy again counted the coins. "I'll have the plain ice cream," he said. The waitress brought the ice cream, put the bill on the table and walked away. The boy finished the ice cream, paid the cashier and departed.

When the waitress came back, she began wiping down the table and then swallowed hard at what she saw. There, placed neatly beside the empty dish were two nickels and five pennies—her tip.

That little boy sure understood the importance of saying *thank you*! It is my wish that every child grows up feeling the importance of saying *thank you* beyond "when mind your manners" is said.

———

Why is it so important to say *thank you* to others? Let me count the reasons. At the top of the list is the fact that happiness in relationships is a predictor of a healthy well-being, more than material possessions. As stated in chapter five, if you don't have your health, nothing else matters. And, in chapter one, if your thoughts and words are positive, you attract the same to you.

Saying *thank you* to others has a multiplier effect. Once you get going with this habit, there are so many more reasons to continue. Acknowledging people reduces the tendency to be judgmental and critical. And, expressing appreciation helps build or increase a healthy sense of community, whether it is within your family, at the workplace or beyond.

I know. You may be saying that there are times when your appreciation or acknowledgment of someone doesn't seem to matter. You may be thinking: *Why bother?* Keep in mind, it's not so much about them as it is about you. For example, when I walk down the street and say hello to someone who doesn't give me a response, I don't take it personally. Greeting the person keeps me smiling, continues my practice of noticing others and maintains my *thank you* consciousness. Acknowledging others ultimately is an investment in YOU.

Similarly, in any situation, if communication with others feels disconnected, critical or judgmental, be the one to initiate a change by expressing those two simple words, *thank you*. If you haven't been saying *thank you* to others lately, start giving out the gold stars now. There are so many ways to do so.

Write "belated *thank you*" letters, deliver them in person or read them over the phone if possible. Remember Charles Plum who learned the value of acknowledging folks behind the scenes. And, no *thank you* idea is too big or impossible as Shauna Fleming and Morrill Worcester demonstrate with their *thank you* campaigns for military personnel.

The key to saying *thank you* to others is to practice with every possible opportunity. Wake up with the intention that you are going to make someone's day each time you say, *thank you*. Every time you do, it will definitely make yours! And, remember:

Expressing your appreciation
to family, friends and folks galore,
Connects you heart to heart
and gives you so much more.

What that is and how it feels
are your gifts to find out,
When you say thank you to others
it works wonders without a doubt!

And now, onward with the advanced practice of saying *thank you!*

....*Notes*

Activities

1. If you have been practicing the art of saying *thank you* with notes to others, have you considered sending a follow up *thank you* at a later date to tell the giver about the joy you have received from their gift? Here is an example of that kind of a *thank you* note to my sister:

Dear Susie,

When you gave me the Queen of Sisters figurine for my birthday a few years ago, I was so touched by the sentiment. I have always made sure that "she" was in a special place to enjoy her dazzling delight. My favorite time is at night when a votive candle lights up the cut-out hearts in her skirt casting dancing hearts on the wall.

I love how the Queen of Sisters resembles me and how the little gold wires come out of her shoulders like angel wings. She is so dear to me and so are you. I just had to tell you again and say thank you with all my heart for this precious gift.

I love you!

Cheryl

Artwork: Courtesy of a huge thank you before I momentarily traded the keyboard for a felt tip pen.

2. Make it a habit of looking at name badges worn by cashiers at retailers and restaurants as well as those of service personnel. Take an extra minute to say *thank you* using the person's name. When you are doing business by phone, jot down the person's name to thank them at the end of the call.

3. While the words, *thank you*, may be universally understood, learning to say *thank you* in other languages such as gracias (Spanish) and merci (French) is a thoughtful gesture to extend. To help you, Google the phrase: *thank you* in other languages. According to Jennifer's language page, there are 465 translations! And, there are more than 30 articles about saying *thank you* in other countries. Enjoy!

At the Workplace

Start a *thank you* campaign at your workplace. Create a form that co-workers can use to write their *thank you* notes or let people use their own creativity. Set up a system for distribution that works such as through inter-office mail, leaving notes on a co-worker's desk or delivering notes in person. If there is room in the employee lunch area or lounge, add a bulletin board for people to leave acknowledgments for one another.

Managers and supervisors are encouraged to say *thank you* regularly, express appreciation frequently. Why wait for the annual review to say *thank you* for a job well done?

References & Resources

Books

Bob Nelson
   1001 Ways to Reward Employees

Pat Williams with Jim Denney
   How to Be Like Walt

Thank You Notes

Bookkeepers/CPAs

I am grateful for your business
each year I do your tax return,
Thank you for your confidence
that I continue striving to keep and earn.

Hairstylists

I love to cut and style hair
that is very clear,
It wouldn't be as much fun
if YOU weren't here looking in the mirror.

I created this little note
and wrote this special rhyme,
To let you know of my appreciation
when you call for an appointment time!

Managers

This company would not be the same
if your name couldn't be found,
Your attention to details and friendly smile
is what helps make our world go 'round.

I created this little note
and wrote this special rhyme,
To let you know of my appreciation
for your dedication and valuable time.

Real Estate Agents

The listing of your home to sell
is now in my professional care,
I thank you for the trust you placed
here's to a deal that's more than fair!

Websites

Andre Agassi's farewell speech
    www.latimes.com/tennis

A Million Thanks
    www.amillionthanks.org

Donors Choose
    www.donorschoose.org

Bob Nelson
    www.nelson-motivation.com

Thank You **Quotes**

Anonymous: *I would say thank you from the bottom of my heart, but for you my heart has no bottom.*

Ron Atchison: *How many times have we walked by someone on the street or in a hallway and instead of saying hello we pretend we don't see them? The truth is that all of us, deep down inside, have a need to be seen, acknowledged and appreciated. We are on a spiritual journey that can at times be very lonely. And one of the simplest and most effective ways to help our fellow traveler is to smile and say hello.*

Louise Caudill: *As I learn to perceive all the gifts with which I am blessed, I become blessed anew. When I recognize and thank Sources of these gifts, I receive even more. When I remember to give constantly, great volumes of riches wait in front of me.*

John F. Kennedy: *As we express our gratitude, we must never forget that the highest appreciation is not to utter words, rather to live by them.*

Christiane Northrup: *Feeling grateful or appreciative of someone or something in our life actually attracts more of the things that you appreciate and value into your life.*

Marcel Proust: *Let us be grateful to the people who make us happy—they are the charming gardeners who make our souls blossom.*

Albert Schweitzer: *At times our own light goes out and is rekindled by a spark from another person. Each of us has cause to think with deep gratitude of those who have lighted the flame within us.*

Seneca: *There is as much greatness of mind in acknowledging a good turn, as in doing it.*

G. B. Stern: *Silent gratitude isn't much use to anyone.*

Henry Van Dyke: *Gratitude is the inward feeling of kindness received, thankfulness is the natural impulse to express that feeling.*

William Arthur Ward: *Feeling gratitude and not expressing it is like wrapping a present and not giving it.*

Say thank you to the birds
say it to the bees,
Say it gratefully especially when
you "see the forest through the trees!"

How to Say *Thank You* with Faith

Faith. What exactly is it?

According to Corrie ten Boom, "Faith sees the invisible, believes the unbelievable and receives the impossible." In Bible scripture, "Faith is the assurance of things hoped for, the conviction of things not seen."

As a little girl, I looked forward to reciting the *Prayer of Faith* with my mom before I went to sleep. When I was a teenager, I learned that if I "had faith the size of a mustard seed, all things are possible." Believing I could "muster" up a little faith when I needed it, I bought a necklace with a mustard seed pendant as a reminder. Between the mustard seed and reciting the *Prayer of Faith*, I thought I had faith.

As adults, we tell each other to "keep the faith" or "have faith." Recognizing that there had to be more to having faith than just believing in it, I was determined to find out how to put faith into action—to really live in a spirit of faith.

My ability to put faith into action increased when I discovered a strong visual in this statement: "Faith is the bridge between fear and action." Now I had a mental picture that helped me be less fearful and take more action in challenging situations. As I increased my practice in the art of saying *thank you*, I took this statement one step further and substituted the word faith with the words, thank you. Finally, I felt I had the tool I needed to live in faith, which I define simply as the ability to "see the forest through the trees."

Saying *thank you* for something beyond what I can see is how I am able to "believe in the assurance of things hoped for and the conviction of things not seen." I say *thank you* as if I already have what I need, want or desire.

From a business perspective, I was taught something similar as a sales rep for Xerox Corporation—to assume the sale until told otherwise. In my professional life, it was easy to "assume the sale." It has taken more practice in my personal life.

My faith in saying *thank you* for what I cannot see has transformed my life in every way. Financial needs have been met, health challenges overcome and dreams manifested. I have experienced "receiving the impossible" many times. All because I said *thank you* for something I could not see.

When I truly trust the process of "believing the unbelievable," the details come together beyond what I can imagine as this story illustrates:

It was a "blue moon" on Sunday, June 30, 1996, the day I moved to a two-bedroom, two-bath, two-car garage house situated on a private lake with ducks and white swans. I felt as if I was living in what I call Mother Nature's Disneyland.

Friends and family were thrilled for me especially since I had lived in less than 200 square feet for 12 years. For that period of time, space didn't matter; the 180 degree ocean view is what counted. Now I had both a spacious home and a water view from every room in this leased home. I was in heaven!

Nine years later in 2005, I was on my way to meet a regional bank president with the executive director of the non-profit organization where I worked. My cell phone rang and it was a call from the owner of my cherished home. Regretfully, she was giving me a 60-day notice because she and her husband decided to move into the house. I had until May 7 to relocate.

I was in shock. I asked if there was any way I could have more time because I had a huge fund-raising event on May 19. Impossible. They had already sold their home in Idaho and things were moving rather quickly. Way too fast for me at that moment. Somehow, I thanked her for letting me know and hung up.

During the next few weeks, I put the idea of moving on the back burner. As the reality sunk in, I knew it was time to look for a new place to live. In my initial search, nothing came close to the housing I had for comparable rent.

The clock was ticking, the owners were concerned and everyone kept asking me where I was going to live. That is when I wrote a *thank you* letter in faith for a new residence. Since I believe in a higher power, I wrote the following *thank you* letter on April 14, 2005:

Dear God,

Thank you for my new place to live. I love it so much!
1. *Thank you for the gorgeous ocean view.*
2. *Thank you for the peaceful sounds of silence.*
3. *Thank you for the fresh, clean feeling of my home.*
4. *Thank you that my furniture fits perfectly.*
5. *Thank you for the birds and gentleness around me.*
6. *Thank you for the great outdoors for my daily walks.*
7. *Thank you for the friendly neighborhood.*
8. *Thank you for the home that feels SO magical!*
9. *Thank you for the affordable rent.*
10. *Thank you for a May 7, 2005 move-in date.*
   With love and hugs,

   Cheryl

As you can see, I was quite specific with everything I wanted to have and feel about my new home. After I wrote my *thank you* note, I was much more focused in my approach to finding a new place to live—another benefit of putting my "*thank you*" faith in writing.

Since an ocean view was a top priority, I determined which cities on the beach were within comfortable driving distance to my job. Next, during a walk on my favorite stretch of beach in north Laguna, I made a mental note about the mobile home park located above Pacific Coast Highway (PCH). *What would it be like to live there?* I decided to find out.

The following day I called the office even though I knew there was litigation between the park residents and the state of California. The lease had not been renewed and the residents were given notice to leave because of plans to build a public campground. I spoke with Kim, a very nice lady who was unable to offer much hope due to the uncertainty of the legal proceedings.

On April 26 while I was driving north on PCH, I saw the entrance to the mobile home park known as El Morro Village in Crystal Cove State Park. I pulled in, parked my car and met Kim who was in the office. We talked briefly since she was ready to leave for the day. Initially Kim said there was nothing available. Remembering my Xerox training, as I was leaving I asked once more about a rental. This time she said #159 might be a possibility. She told me she would let me know, however, I did not hear from Kim the remainder of the week.

On Saturday, April 30 I checked emails to see if there were any housing referrals from my networking efforts. YES! A real estate agent sent me a new studio listing in Laguna Beach. Excited, I drove to the address and waited for the owner. When I saw the rental, it was perfect for someone other than me.

Convinced there was a place for me to live near the ocean, I sat in my car and kept saying *thank you* for my new home. The more I affirmed this, the more empowered I felt.

While I was still sitting in my car, the owner of my current home called and asked if I had found a new place to live. Even though I didn't have one at that moment, I assured her I would move out by the agreed upon date. After the phone call, I drove north on PCH, and once again, there was the mobile home park on my right.

Without even thinking whether the office was open on the weekend or that I hadn't heard from Kim, I turned into the parking lot. The office was open, and there I was introducing myself to Sharon who was working that day. I told her I was there to rent #159. She called the manager as if it had already been arranged. Remember "assume the sale until told otherwise?"

The manager also acted as if #159 was mine telling me the rental would be week to week because of the pending litigation. When I agreed to the terms, she called Bob, chief of maintenance, who took me to see #159. My heart was pounding as I took out my *thank you* letter to "compare notes." Here is what greeted me:

1. **The gorgeous ocean view**

   A full 180 degrees! Straight ahead was Catalina Island, Palos Verdes to the north and the coastline went for miles looking south.

2. **The peaceful sounds of silence.**

   Exquisite. For a Saturday afternoon, everything was so serene and quiet.

3. **The fresh, clean feeling of my home.**

   Even though #159 was at least 35 years old, it was beautifully maintained with red tile floors, freshly painted walls and cupboards...everything was in great condition!

4. **My furniture fits perfectly**

Indeed it did with two bedrooms and two baths. The dining room and living room were large enough for my office as well. Together with the kitchen, they all faced the ocean. Imagine that!

5. **The birds and gentleness around me**

Absolutely!

6. **The great outdoors for my daily walks**

How about miles of beach and acres of canyons?

7. **The friendly neighborhood**

Since Bob was a 30-year resident, he told me about the folks that lived at El Morro Village—the potlucks and events held on the lawn called "the green." He said I would feel like a long-term resident in no time.

8. **The home feels SO magical**

I was ready to move in that day!

9. **The affordable rent**

It was the same as what I had been paying for my home on the lake.

10. **My move-in date is May 7, 2005**

And, of course I did.

The move went easily and effortlessly on May 7. That evening I cooked dinner, lit candles and enjoyed a bubble bath before writing another *thank you* note that sounded very similar to the one I wrote on April 14. The second one had a lot more exclamation points and profuse expressions of gratitude. Otherwise, the description of my home was identical.

The next morning I drove to my mom's house and brought her back to my new home—Starheart by the Sea.

We celebrated Mother's Day as we unpacked a few more items, visited with the first of many friends to stop by, and fixed dinner.

After I took my mom home, I drove back to mine saying *thank you* all the way. With the joy of the day and the feeling I had about realizing my dream home, I smiled at the thought that I would have made the move to have that one day. In my mind, everything else was frosting on the cake.

There was a lot of "frosting" over the next ten months until all residents were required to leave on March 1, 2006. I enjoyed memorable moments with family and friends, spent quiet times on the beach and it was here that I began a daily practice of writing *thank you* notes in the sand. What a thrill to use one of my photographs on the front cover of THANKYOUOLOGY.

The greatest gift I received from living in a trailer park was being reminded of my happiest childhood memories—summer vacations camping in our trailer with my family. I thrived in the great outdoors, and I thrived when I lived in Crystal Cove State Park.

The desire to live and work in another "Mother Nature's Disneyland" was so strong that after I moved out of El Morro Village, I took a 10,000 mile road trip throughout the western United States to research campgrounds, retreat centers and B & B's. This was my first step in realizing a new dream—having a facility to host the ultimate Camp StarHeart for families and individuals. Sounds to me like it is time to write another *thank you* note!

Why is it so beneficial to say *thank you* with faith, to "see the forest through the trees?" When you accept only what you can see or figure out on your own, there is a tendency to accept or settle for less. Dreams and desires of the heart have a difficult time manifesting in a consciousness that has limitations.

What is there to lose in "believing that all things are possible?" The number one answer: You lose your disbelief! Dreams become a reality when fears and disbeliefs give way to taking action, and saying *thank you* with faith is the bridge between the two. When you say *thank you* with faith, you are able to activate what I call the three V's—visualize, verbalize and vitalize.

Using my El Morro story as an example, I visualized my new home in detail. Next, I verbalized with my *thank you* letter and vitalized it by taking action. I "moved my feet" to determine housing possibilities near the ocean, network, follow up on rental ads and stop at El Morro Village.

Reflecting on this experience, I give myself the biggest gold star for asking if there was a rental available even though appearances looked otherwise. Bible scripture tells of the importance to ask, seek and knock. Interesting how the acronym for those three words is: Ask. I believe asking is the key that unlocks all possibilities.

Mark Victor Hansen and Jack Canfield asked many companies to publish *Chicken Soup for the Soul*, the series of books that has become a worldwide phenomenon. More than 30 publishers turned down the idea before the co-authors heard the infamous word: "Yes." Their success story demonstrates the value of having a vision and bridging the vitalization of it with faith. With each "no," I am sure they said *thank you* to a lot of people, and then said, "next," as they moved on.

There are countless stories of people who have turned their dreams into reality. Are they different? Do they have something special? I don't think so. Everyone has the potential to achieve when they believe in the possibility.

Dreams come in all shapes and sizes, and they happen every day depending on your perspective. In my opinion, dreams have no specific definition. Having a good day can be a fulfilled dream if that hasn't been the case for awhile. Your heart's desire is uniquely yours and can be as simple as changing a habit, losing weight, starting a new career or attracting a soul mate. Believing in the vision as a reality is what matters, regardless of the size of the dream.

The manifestation of dreams has its own time line. Some may happen almost overnight, appearing to take the route of a straight line—the shortest distance between two points. Others may travel a path that looks something like a labyrinth with many twists, turns and reversals. Irrespective of the time it takes, believing is the common thread.

To believe "in the appearance of things hoped for, the conviction of things not seen," take your *thank you* affirmations to heart. Use them to write your *thank you* letters with passion and give out the gold stars for every step you take. Use those basic tools and applications to advance your practice of saying *thank you* in ways you never dreamed possible.

You have the ability. I know you do! Whatever you desire, have faith with *thank you* and fortify your spirit with this:

Believe in the power of faith
to reach beyond what you see,
Bridge fear and action with thank you
and use those three words starting with V.

Trust in thank you affirmations
and write those letters too,
The more you practice this principle
the potential is unlimited for you!

....*Notes*

Activities

1. Even though he was bedridden, Walt Disney still shared his dreams by taping them to the ceiling. Because it was difficult for him to talk, Walt asked visitors to sit on his bed to share his latest visions for the future.

   What do you dream of that has not yet manifested? Write a *thank you* note as if you already have it. Do this for every need, dream or heart's desire. Put the *thank you* notes on the ceiling, if you wish.

2. In Jim Stovall's book, *The Ultimate Gift*, he suggests making a dream board with pictures, keywords etc. This is a good place for your *thank you* notes. *Thank you*, Greg, for sharing this book with me.

3. Create a vision circle with family members for a family vacation or other goals and cheer each other on with daily *thank you* sessions.

4. In Shel Silverstein's poem, *What If*, he humorously dialogues about worries. For reference, this poem is on the internet, and in a 20th anniversary edition of his book, *A Light in the Attic*. Another way to dream big is to flip that "what if" question from a negative to a positive. For example:

   What if I quit my job and followed my heart?

   What if I sold my house and sailed around the world?

   What if I wrote a book or made a movie?

   When you are willing to ask "what if" questions about your desires, you make it possible to see what answers you back.

At the Workplace

Companies have visions for future growth and development. Achieving those goals can be faster and easier with everyone on board. Regardless of what position you hold in a company, you can be a key player in the realization of a goal. Be a cheerleader and show what it looks like to believe in things, even if they aren't visible yet.

References & Resources

Books

Jim Stovall
The Ultimate Gift

Prayer of Faith by Hannah Moore Kohaus

God is my help in every need;
God does my every hunger feed;
God walks beside me, guides my way
Through every moment of the day.

I now am wise, I now am true.
Patient, kind, and loving, too.
All things I am, can do and be,
Through Christ the truth that is in me.

God is my health, I can't be sick;
God is my strength unfailing quick;
God is my all, I know no fear,
Since God and love and truth are here.

Thank You Quotes

Martin Luther King: *Take the first step in faith—you don't have to see the whole staircase, just take the first step.*

The Christian Science Monitor: *True gratitude comes even before the events to which it is related.*

> *Be thankful for the raindrops*
> *and loud and roaring thunder,*
> *Now this may somewhat surprise you*
> *say thank you for a "blunder!"*

How to Overcome Challenges Saying *Thank You*

Blunder. A synonym for accident, major heartache, disaster, the worst of the worst. How in the world could a person ever say *thank you* for any or all of that?

In *The Simple Abundance Journal of Gratitude*, Sarah Ban Breathnach writes: "It's easy to be grateful when life hums. Ironically, gratitude's most powerful mysteries are often revealed when we are struggling in the midst of personal turmoil... gratitude holds us together even as we are falling apart."

In 1914, after much of his life's works went up in flames, Thomas Edison remarked: "There is great value in disaster. All our mistakes are burned up. Thank God we can start anew." Three weeks later he delivered the first phonograph.

Deepak Chopra states in his book, *Creating Affluence*: "In every failure is the seed of success. Our failures are stepping stones in the mechanics of creation, bringing us ever closer to our goals. In reality, there is no such thing as failure. What we call failure is just a mechanism through which we can learn to do things right."

Typical reactions to feelings of failure are anger, fear, hate and/or resentment. If Deepak Chopra's suggestion is true that failure is feedback, then negative feelings about a failure are reduced or eliminated. Practicing his advice, I found that I moved forward faster and easier clearing the way for me to think about new directions, choices or options.

I believe singer and actress, Jennifer Hudson, is an excellent role model for Deepak Chopra's definition of failure. Prior to winning an Academy Award for her supporting role in the movie, *Dreamgirls*, she was one of ten finalists on the television show, *American Idol*. During an episode, Judge Simon Cowell told her she "did not have what it takes to be a successful singer." The next night Jennifer Hudson was voted off the show.

Following her rise to fame, Simon Cowell's remarks were a frequent topic of discussion during her first interviews. Publicly, she never expressed anger or feelings that she had failed on *American Idol*. She said when she was voted off the show, she "trusted God had something even greater for her." Jennifer Hudson was able to say *thank you* for the *American Idol* experience just as much as she was able to express her gratitude for the *Dreamgirls* opportunity.

In Alan Cohen's book, *I Had it All the Time*, he writes how every detail of our lives eventually fits into a bigger picture. While the piece we currently experience may be very challenging, ultimately there is wholeness. Frank Slazak discovered how this truth works in the following story:

For 25 years Frank Slazak was a teacher with a life-long dream—to be an astronaut and fly on a mission to outer space. In 1985, NASA announced the Teachers in Space program and he knew this was a chance for his dream to come true. He applied, made it through all of the screenings and was in the final group of 100 aspirants from which one teacher would be selected.

When Christa McAuliffe was chosen to be the Teacher in Space, he was devastated. He could not understand why he was not chosen. On January 28, 1986, when the Challenger exploded 73 seconds after lift off, he had his answer. Today, Frank Slazak is a motivational speaker who shares his belief that every experience is a gift.

So, if what could be called failure is actually feedback,

and if everything experienced fits into a bigger picture of wholeness, then is it possible to say *thank you* in the face of heartbreak, illness, injury, loss or tragedy? It was time for me to find out.

I lived in an apartment complex and my new car was vandalized by a neighbor. It certainly was a horrible shock to have someone deliberately damage my car. The following Sunday I was a guest speaker at the Unity Church in Covina, California. I told the congregation how I was saying *thank you* to focus my attention on the bigger picture rather than the unpleasant piece I had experienced. A month later I moved to the beautiful home I described in the previous chapter. I had driven by that development for three years wondering what it would be like to live there. What a thrill it was to find out—all because my car had been vandalized!

When I heard that my mom fell and broke her hip, it was challenging to think how this would affect her future health and way of life. Once again, I chose to say *thank you* having no idea what the bigger picture was with this experience. The journey with her healing and subsequent health challenges has given me one of the most treasured chapters in my life—easily the topic of another book.

As I practice this concept of a *thank you* consciousness, I find stories where others are also able to say *thank you* even for a "blunder."

In the February 2007 issue of the *Daily Word* magazine, a woman wrote to share her story about a series of events that helped her gain new insight about when to say *thank you*. She called Silent Unity for prayer after the birth of her second daughter who was born with breathing problems. The person on the line responded with a prayer: *Thank you* God for healing and protecting her. The mother wrote that she didn't understand why anyone would say, *thank you*. She was angry and hung up.

When the diagnosis wasn't good and she was told not

to touch her daughter, in desperation she remembered the Unity prayer. She decided to say *thank you* for the health and well-being of her daughter. Soon after she expressed her gratitude, she learned her daughter might benefit from a new FDA approved drug. With its use, her daughter fully recovered within a few weeks.

After this same lady lost her job, she called Silent Unity, and again, the person praying with her gave thanks. This time she knew that by saying *thank you*, there was greater opportunity for new possibilities beyond what she could see at the moment. The key she said was saying *thank you* even in the face of despair.

In May 2007, the *Los Angeles Times* published a front-page column about a very well-known biblical scholar in Pasadena, California. Entitled, *Rejoice Always*, it told how this man was challenged by a particular Bible verse until he was diagnosed with cancer. Finally, the scripture in 1 Thessalonians made sense to him. It states: "Rejoice always, pray continually, give thanks in all circumstances." He said he gave thanks he could still work, be with his family and survive what often felt like challenging medical treatments. He found it possible to "give thanks in all circumstances."

Taro Gold, a young philosopher describes how he learned this same lesson in his book, *Wabi Sabi*. He shares an experience that happened while he and his Japanese mentor, Obaa-san, were shopping at an open air market. A scuffle amongst several men and a shopkeeper escalated to the point that one man carelessly bumped into Obaa-san, lost his balance and tripped over a display of wooden boxes. He shouted profanities at her and stormed off as if it were all her fault. Obaa-san's reaction was to bow and say, *thank you*.

When Taro Gold asked why she said *thank you*, her response was that she did not want to react with more abuse. Rather than plant seeds of turmoil, she wanted to harvest seeds that brought her peace.

W Mitchell (there is no period after the W and he just likes to be called Mitchell) has also demonstrated the ability to be at peace in the face of adversity. I had the privilege of sitting in the front row when he made a guest appearance to talk about his book—*It's Not What Happens to You, It's What You Do About It.* I was profoundly moved by his story.

As he sat in a wheelchair, he told the audience that until the age of 27, his life was one joy ride after another, particularly when he rode his motorcycle or flew his airplane. Then one day he was speeding through an intersection on his motorcycle. He had a terrible accident that hospitalized him for months with third degree burns over more than 70 percent of his body. When he recovered, his hands were stubs, his face was disfigured and he had chronic pain. And yet, he told the audience he was grateful to have survived.

The experience taught him that it is not what happens in life; it is what we do about it. With that kind of attitude, he went on to become mayor of a town in Colorado, build successful businesses and eventually with the use of electronic controls, he was able to pilot an airplane again—his greatest love.

Continuing his story, he asked the audience to imagine what he felt the day he was taking off in his plane and realized it was not going to clear the mountain range ahead of him. Because there was not enough lift, the plane crashed. While the three other passengers were able to free themselves and walk away, Mitchell said he could not feel his legs. That is why he sat before me in a wheelchair.

I marveled at what he had done with his life after two major catastrophes in four years. What I came away with that evening was the reminder that gratefulness takes us so much further than anger, resentment, hate or fear.

Aha! There it is. None of these stories address what to do with the emotional charge (unreleased adrenaline) caused by feelings of anger, resentment, hate and fear that are natural reactions when tough stuff happens. Am I suggesting that these feelings are to be ignored as if nothing happened? Absolutely not, especially since medically speaking, unreleased adrenaline from an emotional charge causes pain, illness, disease or unusual behavior.

A segment of the television show, *60 Minutes* that aired in 2007, confirmed in its report that excessive adrenaline is definitely damaging to the body. Of particular focus was how excessive adrenaline is a cause of post-traumatic stress. The news feature reported on a new drug that has helped people regain their physical and emotional lives because it reduces the excess adrenaline in the body.

Since I prefer holistic alternatives, I would like to say a special *thank you* to Sherie Kennedy who is a gifted healer, counselor and author of *A Tool Book—Assisting Conscious Awareness.* I am grateful to her for teaching me how to release an emotional charge, which in turn releases excess adrenaline. I call her life-changing technique the triple A's, which means to acknowledge, allow and accept. With her permission, the following is an excerpt from her book describing this powerful emotional release method.

"The emotions of hate, anger, fear and resentment are neutral; it's the charge that creates a positive or negative effect. Anger can be violent and destructive or it can motivate tremendous change. Fear can paralyze your ability to act or it can save your life. It's not the emotion; it's what you do with it.

"The emotion either controls you or you control it. You control it by acknowledging, allowing and accepting it. When you do that it returns to the love from which it came. To deny, negate, ignore, or resist the emotion, and any of the adjectives used to describe it, guarantees it will control you.

"The way to release a charge is to acknowledge what you feel, allow your body to feel it (the adrenaline), and accept that it's okay to feel it (your feelings). This is not about the experience; it is about your feelings toward the experience.

"Again, when you feel hate, anger, fear or resentment, in any form, you are in a charge and it must be released to regain balance. Here's how:

"**First,** say verbally, 'I feel <u>fill in the emotion</u>.'

"**Second,** feel the sensation of adrenaline in your body then feel it leaving your body through your feet.

"**Third,** let it be okay to feel it – why wouldn't you feel what you're feeling?

"It's a one-step, three-part process, and the minute you do it, you'll feel a release in your body."

––––––

Using the triple A's has enabled me to reframe experiences that I originally thought were negative in some way. No matter when they occurred in my life, the emotional charge can be cleared at any time. The key is recognizing that a charge exists by paying attention to pain, illness, injury or changes in behavior. For example, with the triple A's, I healed from the chronic emotional symptoms of a terrifying car accident at 16 years of age and subsequent physical pain that two back surgeries did not correct.

Now I know that if I stuff feelings, and act as if I don't feel them, the unresolved turmoil keeps me stuck in the past, unable to move forward. And, anytime I feel pain or other discomfort in my body, that's a red flag telling me there is excess adrenaline from emotions I did not acknowledge, allow and accept. Recognizing feelings of anger, resentment, hate and fear is a vital tool to regain my balance from the emotional charge of an experience, and live more in the present moment.

It's an ongoing journey practicing the triple A's to release feelings of anger, fear, hate or resentment. Of these four emotions, the one that has tripped me up the most is fear, and even a "fear of fear." To help me acknowledge, allow and accept this emotion, I wrote a poem that I am sharing with you in the chapter Notes. I would also like to share a story of how I used the triple A's to release fear and anger from an experience that had an incredible impact on the writing of THANKYOUOLOGY.

It had been a long session at the computer when suddenly the text was deleting like quicksand, making it difficult to save the document. After I managed to do so, everything was gone when I reopened it.

My first reaction was shock that something like this could happen while I was writing the book of my dreams! It took me awhile to go beneath the feeling of shock and recognize the emotional charge of anger and fear. I acknowledged, allowed and accepted my feelings. For me, tears are a signal I have successfully completed the process. Sometimes there is laughter or I feel a tingling sensation. A physical shift signifies that feelings and excess adrenaline have been released.

Once I cleared the emotional charge, I did two things: Took my laptop in to be checked and repeatedly said *thank you* to see the gifts of this experience. There were several.

First, I realized I needed to change how I was saving my work to safeguard against losing unsaved text. Next, I reflected on how the copy deleted itself since it never happened before and hasn't happened since! I asked myself if I was thrilled with how things were going or was the "disappearing text" a metaphor of something I did not want to see or feel. To find out, I took a break for a few days—went on walks, worked on a few art projects and kept saying *thank you*.

When I was ready to see "what was what" with THANKYOUOLOGY, I used *thank you* affirmations to start my writing session. Immediately, fresh ideas came to me easily and effortlessly. Chapters were rearranged and the format of the book took on a whole new look. Nothing was "lost" and everything worthwhile was "saved" in an exciting new version.

From this experience, I gained a better understanding of Edison's opinion that "there is great value in disaster" because I have found it does give me a chance to "start anew." That is what I am offering in this chapter—tools to start anew, to move forward after any situation that looks or feels like a "blunder."

I believe people who turn adversity into triumph use mental tools to deal with the gamut of emotions that are natural with challenges such as a tragedy, loss, disaster or life-threatening diagnosis. They are like the caterpillar that goes into the cocoon and emerges as a butterfly. With faith to let go of the past, they make the transformation in their thoughts and actions to realize a new beginning. Saying *thank you* is an excellent tool to help you make that change when the need arises. To be clear, saying *thank you* is to focus your mind on the present to access new possibilities; it is not said in response to the unfortunate details of an experience.

Positive psychologists agree that a gratitude consciousness "in all circumstances" is the best way to maintain mental, physical, emotional and spiritual health. I think Psychologist Philip Watkins, professor at Eastern Washington University, sums it up best: "Thankfulness helps the brain fully process events. Grateful people achieve closure by making sense of negative events so that they mesh with a generally positive outlook." To that I would like to add:

> Whenever a "blunder" occurs
> release the emotions galore,
> Then, the way is cleared for you
> to say thank you and open a new door!

....*N*otes

Activities

1. Make a collage using a combination of "blunder" words and the words, *thank you*. Use colors and pictures to be creative. Put copies in your purse or briefcase, on the bathroom mirror, in the car and at work to remind you that in any negative situation, you can say *thank you* once you have acknowledged, allowed and accepted your feelings.

2. Watch for articles in the newspaper or magazines about people who overcome adversity with a positive approach. Cut them out and make a collection as a reminder of how you can do the same with a *thank you* consciousness.

3. Journal about acknowledging, allowing and accepting your feelings of fear, anger, resentment or hate. Poems and artwork help you talk out these feelings and let them go. That is how my drawing of "Little Cheryl" was created.

4. Reflect on past experiences that have felt like a mistake, blunder, tragedy or worse such as a car accident, divorce, loss of a loved one, a dream that didn't materialize. Next, make two lists—the first is for

situations that you already see how there was a hidden gift. On the other list, describe events that still hurt, feel awful, etc. One at time, see if you can release any feelings of anger, fear, resentment or hate with the triple A's. Take your time with this activity.

At the Workplace

The art of saying *thank you* is an excellent tool for crisis management. This is a time when management can take the lead in redirecting concerns and fears about something that has had a negative impact on the financial structure, company culture or operations.

People become stronger in times of trouble when given the opportunity to work together toward the solution. Be the one to suggest a gratitude consciousness at the beginning of problem-solving discussions.

If employees have to be laid off, this can be done with respect and dignity. If relocation of the business is involved, orchestrating the process with gratitude will reap far better returns than with anger, hate, resentment and fear.

It only takes one person who believes in the power of *thank you* to be the catalyst for a positive approach to any situation. Be that person!

References & Resources

Books

Deepak Chopra
  Creating Affluence

Alan Cohen
  I Had It All the Time

Taro Gold
  Wabi Sabi

Sherie Kennedy
  A Tool Book: Assisting Conscious Awareness

W Mitchell
It's Not What Happens to You,
It's What You Do About It

Poem About Fear

Yes, I have fears
and yes, anxiety too,
I acknowledge, allow and accept
to laugh or cry "boo hoo."

How new for me to say
if I am scared and unsure,
How grand for me to accept
what's been hard to endure.

It's only my judgment or comparison
that make these feelings wrong,
Now I say thank you, and
write a rhyme or sing a song.

I am so grateful
that I can finally see,
How expressing my feelings
helps me let go of fear and anxiety.

Thank You Quotes

Melody Beattie: *Gratitude unlocks the fullness of life. It turns what we have into enough, and more. It turns denial into acceptance, chaos into order and confusion into clarity. It can turn a meal into a feast, a house into a home, a stranger into a friend. Gratitude makes sense of our past, brings peace for today and creates a vision for tomorrow.*

Sarah Ban Breathnach: *Let your thanksgiving for all that is rise above the din of disappointment— opportunities lost, mistakes made, the clamor of all that has not yet come.*

Cicero: *Gratitude is not only the greatest of virtues, but the parent of all the others.*

Alan Cohen: *Converting your focus of energy from criticism to gratitude will change your life forever.*

Alex Haley: *Find the good and praise it.*

Helen Keller: *I thank God for my handicaps, for through them I have found myself, my work, my God.*

Dawna Markova: *Gratitude is like a flashlight. If you go out in your yard at night, suddenly you can see what's there when you turn on a flashlight. It was always there, but you couldn't see it in the dark.*

Peter Marshall: *A prayer...let us not be frightened by the problems that confront us, rather give Thee thanks that Thou hast matched us with this hour. May we resolve, God helping us, to be part of the answer, and not part of the problem. Amen.*

Geshe Michael Roach: *Pain can have the greatest potential for us to discover the laws of hidden potential. It is the best thing that ever could have happened to us.*

Chapter 9

*In case you haven't noticed
saying thank you requires no special tools,
Remember the first rule is
that's just it...there are no rules!*

How to Express *Thank You* Your Way

Tools? Rules?

Whenever I hear something that doesn't make sense to me, I ask the question: Who wrote that rule? For example, just because there is a saying, "You can't have your cake and eat it too," doesn't make it a rule. My response is: Why have the cake if you can't eat it?

In lieu of specific rules or requirements, I have shared the tools and resources I use to live the art of saying *thank you* as a guide for your own expression of a philosophy I call THANKYOUOLOGY. To further help you say *thank you* your way, I offer more of my favorite *thank you* ideas:

Gratitude Businesses

If you live in the San Francisco area, enjoy a visit to one of the Café Gratitude restaurants where "food and people are a celebration of our aliveness" according to the founders, Terces and Matthew Engelhart. The company's website is worth a visit to see its magical interpretation of the phrase, "a world of plenty."

Are you aware of the 42-day GoGratitude (not a typo) Experiment? Nearly 200,000 people from 153 countries have joined and over a million people have watched the GoGratitude Flash movie since Stacey Robyn first launched it in 2005. On the website listed in the chapter Notes is a three-minute video that shows how a common symbol of gratitude is evident in the earth, plants, water, stars and more. It gives a powerful perspective on the magnitude of gratitude.

Resignation Letters with Gratitude

When I decided to tender a letter of resignation, I put my thoughts of appreciation and dreams for the future into a poem that I read to my boss. It turned out to be an unforgettable experience for both of us, and it sure made the conversation about leaving a lot easier. This is what I said:

> *Today I am so grateful*
> *for the light that has helped me see,*
> *To give my notice, make the space*
> *for all I believe is meant for me.*
>
> *My goals are simple, yes they are*
> *to feel energy, excitement and more,*
> *To be of service with a smile*
> *using my creative ideas galore.*
>
> *It has been said about baseball*
> *that you can't get to second base,*
> *If you don't take your foot off first*
> *I know for a fact that is the case.*
>
> *I have accomplished a lot in my career*
> *I think there's more big "hits" for me,*
> *I see some home runs for sure, and*
> *I am grateful for those I hit at HRC.*
>
> *So with sincere appreciation*
> *I say thank you with all my heart,*
> *I am open to working out the details*
> *of how I will say goodbye and depart.*

Thank You Themed Bulletin Boards

If you have the space at home or at work, set up a bulletin board to post *thank you* sayings, articles, poems and other gratitude expressions. There are wonderful stories in newspapers and magazines worth saving as reminders about the benefits of thinking, saying and acting with a *thank you* consciousness. For those with space challenges, creating a notebook is a good substitute for this activity.

Up the Down *Thank You* Staircase

When you are going up or down stairs, say *thank you* with each step. Surprising how fast you get up the stairs. If you are climbing a hill, extend your arms as if someone is pulling you up, smile and say *thank you* all the way!

Automotive *Thank You*'s

When starting your car, say *thank you*. When you get where you are going, say *thank you*. If you wash your own car, use the time to acknowledge it. As I am washing the wheels, I say *thank you* to the tires for getting me to my destinations safely. Washing the windows, I acknowledge the benefit of seeing clearly as I am driving. Time polishing the hood is spent expressing gratitude for the engine and everything else that keeps running so beautifully. I also say *thank you* to my car with regular oil changes every 3,500 miles.

Waiting to Say *Thank You*

Even though we seem to excel at multi-tasking, there are times when we have to just wait—sitting at a traffic signal, standing in line, waiting for an appointment. Use the time to think or say, *thank you*.

Household *Thank You*'s

Fixing a meal, washing dishes, cleaning? Each time you do any of these activities say, *thank you*. If you hear yourself grumbling about doing these tasks, say *thank you* to divert your attention to something more enjoyable to think about—what you are looking forward to or reliving a happy memory.

Thank You is Money in the Bank

Writing a check? Depositing a check? I write *thank you* on my checks and draw stars and hearts too!

Find pennies? Nickels? Dimes? Quarters? Dollars? Five's, ten's or twenty's? Say *thank you* every time! As you practice noticing prosperity in this way, you will find it in other areas of your life as well. I put my "monetary finds" in containers to remind me of the abundance all around me.

Every time I spend money, I say *thank you* knowing that as it goes out, it returns to me at least tenfold!

Techno *Thank You*

With the advanced technology for our computers, cell phones, cameras, televisions and more, I think saying *thank you* is vital. Each time my laptop fires right up, I feel grateful. If something becomes a techno challenge, the first thing I do is say *thank you* to keep me calm. Otherwise, getting upset delays the potential for a speedy solution.

Mother Nature *Thank You* Notes

If you live near the ocean, write a person's name in the sand who you would like to send a *thank you* note. Take a photograph to use on the front of a one-of-a-kind note card. This idea also works for writing names in the snow or soil.

I saw a marriage proposal written in the sand with seashells that asked: Will U B My Wife? The words *thank you* can be written with pennies, rocks, leaves or flowers. Match the choice of material to the topic of your note such as pennies if you are saying *thank you* for a financial gift.

Gratitude Books and Letters

Ask family and friends to write what they are thankful for and compile a gratitude book. Or, create your own collection of stories, poems and notes of gratitude about the special people in your life. Online memory books offer a multitude of ideas for this kind of project. For the techno talented, photographs and music can be used to create a gratitude video. Duplicate copies make great gifts.

Classroom Gratitude Projects

I visited an ESL class during the week of Thanksgiving. We talked about the art of saying *thank you* and the teacher asked the students to write their feelings about this quote by Dennis Prager: "Gratitude is the key to happiness." I have included some of their responses (written in their own style) to show the benefits of teaching a gratitude consciousness to our youth.

Adam: "I think this means that if you are thankful for something you should be happy for it. Some people think that money can buy everything. I don't think that you can buy the love of a family member or the love of someone close to you. I think that with every gift comes a reason for happiness."

Alfonso: "I think this means that you have to be thankful for what you have in this life. Some people are sad because they want more of what they have. You have to be grateful for what you have. Each morning when you wake up, the first word that you have to say is thanks to God for letting me live one more day in this life."

Cardena: "If we say the little word, but with a big meaning, it can make others feel good as well as ourselves. Thanks for living, thanks for food to eat, thanks for sleep, thanks for everything. I think if we do that we also learn to say thanks to other people, we will feel peace and happiness."

Jacqueline: "People should appreciate what other people do for them. This is what I think this positive affirmation means."

Johnny: "Well, I guess this guy is trying to say that if you appreciate more things you will be a lot happier with yourself. If you don't appreciate things you will never be happy. It's like my friend Blonka, she is always happy. On the other hand I have this friend named Fernando and he's never happy with anything. You could tell he was an angry person just by the way he carries himself. If you were to see these two people you could tell who appreciates things and who doesn't."

Karen: "Some people have a problem. For one reason they are not happy. They don't know that gratitude is the key to happiness. Happiness is a very important feeling that all people can have. Gratitude is the key that makes them feel happy. Some people have great things that not everyone can have, but they are not happy. They want more but they don't appreciate all the things that they have. For that reason they can't be happy."

Maria: "You have to be thankful for what you have now. I think this is true that gratitude is the key to happiness. I think that Dennis wanted all the people to be thankful of what they have, but I think that is not possible because some people do not believe in gratitude."

Nancy: "Be thankful for what you have, whether it is boring, good or fair. The key to happiness is getting along with everybody, sharing your love with anyone around you and sharing your thoughts, ideas and feelings with the people. Take the right path, not the wrong so later on you don't have to be regretting anything. Other than regretting, just be thankful and always show the positive, not the negative."

Nataly: "I think this statement means that everybody has a key to their own happiness. Gratitude for me means to be thankful for what you have."

Atypical Acknowledgment Announcement

Since there are no rules about where or when to say *thank you*, I decided that here and now is a perfect place to express my acknowledgments for THANKYOUOLOGY. I thought it would be fun to tuck them in an unexpected spot similar to the joy of hiding and finding Easter eggs. Without further ado, I would like to say:

Thank you, Alice, for your humor, heart and incredible patience in addition to your great graphic design talent.

Thank you, Aliana, Caterina, Cindy Lu and Bobby Too, Sherie and Valerie for being there when I called to share the thrills of my writing progress.

Thank you, Clemencia and Joseph, and the caregiving staff at El Descanso residence, for your unconditional love and care of my Mommy Dear, giving me the peace of mind to totally focus on my writing.

Thank you, CZ, for the house sitting opportunity in October 2007 at your casita by the beach. *Thank you*, Yolanda, for giving me your half of the month, making it four fabulous weeks of writing time!

Thank you, Big Sis and King Richard, for the loving and generous hospitality you extended to me while I finished writing THANKYOUOLOGY. And…

Thank you for the power of *thank you* affirmations. I used them constantly to turn the dream of writing this book into a reality.

Thank You Chatter

It occurred to me that this "no rules" chapter is a perfect place to let you hear some of my *thank you* chatter. Contrary to popular belief about talking to ourselves, I talk to myself all the time! In fact, when people ask me about traveling solo around the world, my response is that there were, and still are, three of us: me, myself and I. You can bet there are times when that combination makes for some lively conversations! Here is some of my *thank you* chatter:

1. When there is a near miss of some kind,
    I say *thank you* over and over, in my mind.

2. When I am working with numbers, I say *thank you*
    To definitely avoid a "dyslexic switcheroo."

3. When I remember what I almost forgot,
    I say *thank you*—that's what I've always taught.

4. When I figure out how to fix something,
    saying *thank you* makes my "gold star" bell ring.

5. When plans come together whatever for,
    if they don't, I say *thank you* for the detour.

6. When I save money, it's such a fun surprise,
    saying *thank you* is a big part of the prize.

7. When a magical idea pops into my head,
    I am saying *thank you* until I go to bed.

8. When I think I am done for the day,
    after a burst of energy, *thank you* is what I say.

9. Every time I realize how incredible it is to live,
    saying a heartfelt *thank you* is what I give.

10. When I don't know "what it is"
    only that there is something more,
    I say *thank you*...yes, indeed
    it always opens a brand new door.

I hope hearing some of my random *thank you* chatter and the other ideas in this chapter inspire you to have fun expressing *thank you* your way. There really aren't any rules to do this...just lots of tools from which to pick and choose what works for you. On that note, here is one more thought:

*Be creative and free
let your imagination play,
To discover what happens
when you say thank you your way!*

Activities

1. Make up your own ways to say *thank you*. Remember, there are no rules!

2. See how many ways you can write *thank you* such as:

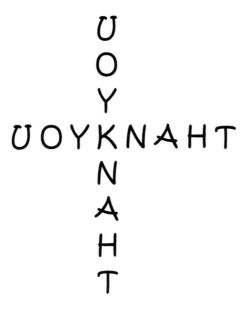

3. When you are reading the newspaper or a magazine, look for the good news stories about people who make the world around them a better place. I have had great success in contacting the writer of the article and obtaining an email address of the person featured in the story. Then, I send that person a *thank you* note letting them know how much I appreciate their efforts. Can you imagine how it feels to receive an acknowledgment from someone you don't know?

    To give you an idea of how this works, I have included some of my favorite stories about people to which I have sent a note of thanks and appreciation.

- When Peg, Patty and Claire Feodoroff put their heads together about the problems with typical hospital gowns, they started a line of gowns to maintain modesty and dignity while undergoing medical visits. www.spirited-sisters.com.

- Rebecca Katz wrote *One Bite at a Time* after her experience of cooking for her father when he had throat cancer. *Thank you*, Rebecca, for taking the time to share with others so lovingly what you have learned. www.onebiteatatime.com.

- In South Central Los Angeles, a group of men in their sixties who were gang members in the 1960's have formed a group called the Businessmen. They act as informal youth counselors and 12-step sponsors to "create a better community by eliminating violence and crime" according to the mission statement of a non profit for which they have applied.

- In China there is a concerned citizen, Chen Si, who patrols the Yanjing Bridge watching for people who look suicidal. According to an article in the Los Angeles Times about his efforts, Chen Si has saved 144 lives as of May 2008.

4. The website, www.myhero.com, is an excellent re-source for stories and videos of people making a difference in their life's work or as volunteers. Taking a few minutes to send some of these folks a *thank you* note or letter of appreciation is a win-win for both you and the recipient.

At the Workplace

Propose having a *thank you* suggestion box giving everyone the opportunity to offer ideas on how to say *thank* you to each other. Give prizes for the funniest, the most motivating, the best results.

References & Resources

Books

Terces and Matthew Engelhart
I Am Grateful

Stacy Robyn
Go Gratitude!

Café Gratitude, LLC

160 14th Street,
San Francisco, CA 94103
Main office: 415-229-7768
info@cafegratitude.com

Locations:
2400 Harrison Street
San Francisco, CA 94110

1336 9th Avenue
San Francisco, CA 94122

1730 Shattuck
Berkeley, CA 94709

2200 4th Street
San Rafael, CA 94901

Websites

www.ExpressGratitude.com

www.GoGratitude .com

Thank You Quotes

Cheryl Russell: *Thank you for the acronym for the word, STOP—See The Other Possibilities.*

Chapter 10

Simply put it's plain to see
saying thank you is an art,
Try it now and see what happens
when you say thank you with all your heart!

How to Receive the Gifts of Saying *Thank You*

Receive. Synonyms are welcome, accept, to be given.

When you say *thank you* with all your heart, the unlimited potential of what you receive is the exciting final chapter of THANKYOUOLOGY. This is where it all comes together because vitalizing your spirit with *thank you* thoughts, words and actions is how you activate the potential to abundantly receive.

Saying *thank you* works both as a way of giving as well as receiving. One is not superior to the other as the saying that "it is better to give than receive" might suggest. Just as breathing requires both inhaling and exhaling, the same is true for giving and receiving. There must be a balance of both. The question is: Are you ready to receive?

To start this discussion, I actually did a search on Google to see what I would find in cyberspace about this topic. Delightfully, I came across a short story that shows how "timing" might play a role in when we are ready to receive. Enocia Joseph shared this story about her mother who was very eager to have surgery for a hip replacement.

When her mother went to the hospital for preliminary tests a month before the scheduled surgery, she was asked if she would like to have her hip replaced that day due to a cancellation. Her response was extreme panic and sky-rocketing blood pressure.

The daughter and her mother had a good laugh

when the mother realized that because she had "planned" to have the hip replacement in another month, she wasn't ready to receive one that day.

An experience that taught me about the importance of being ready to receive happened when I found the mobile home at El Morro Village. For a moment, let's go back to the story in chapter seven because I very carefully left out a small detail. Actually, it was a big one.

After Bob took me up to #159, he encouraged me to get some lunch, return and stay as long as I wished. As I sat on the deck eating my lunch, all I could see was the incredible view of the ocean. Finally, I called my friend, Sherie, to tell her the good news.

Immediately she told me that my voice didn't sound right. She said there was something strange about it. I tried to brush off her comment. Thankfully, good friends don't let you get away with stuff, and she didn't.

With more prodding, I was able to admit that I was afraid of what people would think if I made the move knowing I might have to move again if the pending litigation was unfavorable for the residents. I had so many questions: What about the costs of moving? What about feeling disappointment if I had to leave right away? Was it worth all the hassle? There were plenty of "what ifs."

Finally, I got to the truth. I was feeling afraid to accept something that seemed risky even though the opportunity to rent #159 matched everything in my *thank you* letter about a place to live. I was having a difficult time receiving the abundance of it all.

Recognizing I was emotionally charged by fear, I used the triple A's to acknowledge, allow and accept my feelings. As soon as I released the charge, fear no longer had any power over my decision. Immediately my voice returned to its normal tone and I felt total excitement.

Unconditionally receiving my new home gave me something beyond the ocean view. I never saw the gorgeous palm tree about ten feet from where I was sitting, until the moment I let go of the fear. Previously, I had no idea it was there! The fronds gently waved in the breeze as if they were welcoming me with open arms to my new home. It was so magical!

That precious palm tree became my shoulder to lean on, my rock, my confidante, my mentor. I photographed it from every vantage point and wrote poems expressing my love and appreciation for it. As a "going away" gift to myself, I had a very talented artist capture on canvas the essence of the palm tree and the incredible ocean view. *Thank you*, Steve.

I am grateful for all I received as a resident of El Morro Village—especially the experience of whether or not I was willing to accept the gift of living there in the first place! Since that memorable moment, receiving the vast rewards of saying *thank you* has been more enjoyable than ever!

In the book, *The Art of Receiving*, Sharon Warren asks: "Can you imagine saying *thank you* to God, and God having receiving issues? Can you conceive of God not feeling worthy, or not deserving of your expressions of appreciation? How ludicrous would that be?"

If it has been your nature to tell people that "they shouldn't have" or in any way minimize the joy of receiving, you are shortchanging yourself as well as the giver. When you are given a compliment, graciously say *thank you* without any kind of counter comment to spoil the joy of giving and receiving. Honor the giver and delightfully accept gestures that offer to treat you to a meal or an outing of some kind. In challenging times, trust that people want to do for you what they are offering and allow them to do so!

Sharon Warren also suggests: "Become conscious of opening your heart to receive and don't automatically feel like you have to reciprocate." The movie, *Pay It Forward*, popularized the idea of giving back by paying it forward. For this concept to work, it is necessary to be a good receiver. Otherwise, how can we pay it forward if no one is willing to receive without immediately reciprocating back to the giver?

Admittedly, it took some practice for me to believe that who "I am" is worthy and deserving of receiving abundance without feeling the need to reciprocate to that person in a similar manner. For example, there was a time when I was between jobs, finances were tight and a friend inquired about the amount of my monthly expenses. I told her and a check arrived two days later. As Sharon Warren suggested, imagine if I had turned her gift down or tried to reciprocate with something of equal value? We both would have been shortchanged. *Thank you*, Champe.

Saying *thank you* gives great returns—a healthier body, more harmonious relationships and many dreams fulfilled. Equally valuable are receiving the mental, emotional and spiritual gifts of saying *thank you*. I love it when dots connect in my head giving me those magical mental moments. The feelings I feel, and the self-awareness about who I am and where I am going, is what I love most about practicing the art of saying *thank you*. Seeing over and over how saying *thank you* transforms ANYTHING—physically, mentally, emotionally or spiritually—into something greater, is a most magnificent way of life.

And now, as the conclusion of THANKYOUOLOGY approaches, I think it is fitting for a "conversational text-book" to include a summary of the key points. To that end, there are three highlights for each chapter and a few more perspectives about what happens "when you say *thank you* with all your heart." Are you ready? Then, here we go!

Chapter 1—Thoughts, Words and Actions

Key points:

- Thoughts determine words and actions.

- Of the four agreements, the most important is to be impeccable with your word.

- Meister Eckhart: "If the only prayer you said your whole life was *thank you* that would suffice."

What you receive in life is a direct result of what you think, say and do. *Thank you* thoughts, words and actions, nourish your spirit with light and love. Your life takes on new meaning and purpose when you focus thoughts and energy toward the fulfillment of your spirit. Making a choice to have a *thank you* consciousness is a choice to live a life that thrives!

Chapter 2—*Thank You* Rhymes

Key Points:

- *Thank you* rhymes keep your thoughts in the present moment.

- The rhythm of the rhymes works like songs—they repeat and reinforce the ideas you are imprinting.

- Thinking poetically expands creative thinking and the ability to resolve problems easier.

Thank you rhymes replace "mind chatter" with focused attention giving you a lighter and brighter mental outlook. An optimistic attitude makes it easier to see other options, look at things differently and approach challenging situations with more of an open mind. The ultimate gift of *thank you* rhymes is how they expand your imagination and create dazzling delight in your life.

Chapter 3—*Thank You* Affirmations

Key Points:

- Affirmations empower you to take charge of your life.

- *Thank you* affirmations state the intention and express gratitude at the same time.

- Sources for *thank you* affirmations are: titles of songs, movies, books as well as lyrics, famous dialogue, quotes and most importantly, your own imagination.

The feeling of awe and the joy of receiving occurs every time there is a response to a *thank you* affirmation. It happens when you use them for everything big or small. Whatever the need, *thank you* affirmations work. Just think, with more than 50,000 thoughts a day, the potential benefits from saying *thank you* are rather spectacular!

Chapter 4—*Thank You* Journal

Key Points:

- It is important to acknowledge every step toward goals and accomplishments.

- In the morning, saying *thank you* and affirming intentions in writing focuses the mind and heart for the day.

- In the evening, giving out the gold stars is a personal way to celebrate those magical moments that deserve to be recognized.

The daily routine of a *thank you* journal develops personal discipline and direction. Keeping a record gives you the gifts of reflection, celebration of accomplishments, and the realization of each step as a dream manifests into reality. Because you captured these precious moments in writing, you are able to relive them again and again, and use them as support in the future for going beyond what you can imagine!

Chapter 5—*Thank You* to Your Body

Key Points:

- The body deserves constant acknowledgment, recognition and appreciation.

- Say *thank you* to your body and it will say *thank you* to you with better health and well-being.

- You have the power to say *thank you* from A to Z and from head to toe.

What you receive when you say *thank you* to your body is the ability to take charge of your health and well-being. When you know and appreciate your body for all it does for you, it's impossible to mistreat it in any way. You think kind thoughts, speak loving words and act in positive ways that support your total sense of self. Then, your spirit is unstoppable!

Chapter 6—*Thank You* to Others

Key Points:

- Want to be thanked? Acknowledged? Appreciated? Give what you wish to receive.

- Recognize opportunities to express meaningful appreciation and offer it regularly.

- Saying *thank you* to your family, friends, co-workers and those who "pack your parachute," gives you so much in return.

"The more you give, the more you receive" is especially true for saying *thank you* to others. It is priceless to receive those indescribable feelings that warm your heart and feed your spirit. Creating a seamless cycle of giving and receiving strengthens community spirit for greater understanding and compassion. The support of others cheers you on as well as cheers you up. What a bounty to receive!

Chapter 7—*Thank You* with Faith

Key Points:

- Faith is the bridge between fear and action.

- Substituting the words, *thank you*, for the word faith is how to "see the forest through the trees."

- To actualize your dreams, use the three V's—visualize, verbalize and vitalize.

Every time you say *thank you* for something beyond what you see in the present moment, you gain the confidence to trust and have more faith. This trust and faith gives you the patience to believe in the "conviction of things not seen." Use this power to manifest your dreams with *thank you* affirmations. Take action as a result of your visualizations and reap the rewards of your *thank you* consciousness.

Chapter 8—Overcome Challenges with *Thank You*

Key Points:

- "Gratitude holds us together even when we are falling apart," states Sarah Ban Breathnach.

- Deepak Chopra claims that failure is feedback and Alan Cohen teaches that each experience is part of a bigger picture.

- Releasing the emotional charge of a challenging situation by acknowledging, allowing and accepting the feelings makes it possible to move forward.

The benefits are many for letting go of anger, hate, resentment or fear in challenging circumstances. When the mind is released from holding on to the past or feeling apprehension about the future, saying *thank you* makes it possible to see new options and make new choices. Releasing the emotional charge of a challenging situation lifts the spirit, renews the energy and clears the way to live in the present moment.

Chapter 9—Express *Thank You* Your Way

Key Points:

- When something doesn't quite make sense, ask: Who wrote that rule?

- There are no rules with the art of saying *thank you*.

- Be creative and design your own *thank you* lifestyle.

You have unlimited potential with the art of saying *thank you*. You are the person who determines the use of THANKYOUOLOGY principles. You are free to use and feel the power of saying *thank you* in any way and at anytime! Remember this: There are no rules!

Chapter 10—Receive the Gifts of Saying *Thank You*

Key Points:

- Giving and receiving are circular in the art of saying *thank you*.

- With *thank you* thoughts, words and actions, you concurrently give and receive.

- Thriving on the nourishment of saying *thank you*, your spirit attracts health, wealth, wonderful relationships, success on the job and the manifestation of dreams.

Three words say it all: Receiving is wondrous! The seamless cycle of giving and receiving activated by saying *thank you* feeds the spirit and nurtures the soul. When your spirit is thriving, you are transforming. When you are transforming your life, you are creating a most magnificent way to live!

————

Earlier in this chapter, I said it was most fitting to include a summary in a "conversational textbook" which I think was a win-win: You received the benefit of a review and I received the advantage of reflection. Do you know that a synonym for reflection is manifestation? And, a synonym for manifestation is the word, materialize?

Plenty has materialized since I wrote the introduction for THANKYOUOLOGY. Toward the end of the foreword, I mentioned having "a few more points to make before getting started." The same holds true for my closing remarks. I have a few more points. Specifically, to recap what has materialized since introducing "my story of how, when, where and why to say *thank you* with your thoughts, words and actions."

First, to sum up **how** the art of saying *thank you* works, it is: Saying *thank you* is how to stay in the present moment with a gratitude consciousness and return to it when your attention wanders back to the past or into the future.

You have a destination, a purpose in life. On that journey, stuff happens—big stuff, little stuff and everything in between. Saying *thank you* is what keeps you living in the moment even with bumps or turbulence along the way.

Next, to sum up **when** to say *thank you*, my answer is with one word: Now. Every moment is now. You can't say *thank you* in past moments; you can't say *thank you* in future moments. That means you only have NOW to say *thank you*.

Then, to sum up **where** to say *thank you*, my response is: Wherever you are!

Finally, to sum up **why** to say *thank you*, I have this to declare: Every time you have a *thank you* thought, word or action, you are contributing to a world of love and respect—a world of peace. Saying *thank you* to yourself creates a powerful interconnection between your mind, body and spirit. When you make that connection, you are able to connect with others. People connecting to each other create community. With community, there is love and respect. In an atmosphere of love and respect, there is peace. That is the power of saying *thank you*!

Now, dear person, it is time to take action, to create your own magnificent way of life with the art of saying *thank you*. It's time to write your own story about what happens "when you say *thank you* with all your heart" because:

I know you are ready
to say thank you and receive,
I know you have the tools
that's what I aimed to achieve.

Now it is my pleasure
I just couldn't resist,
To officially bestow upon you
the title of THANKYOUOLOGIST!

Yes, indeed!

....*Notes*

Activities

1. Karen Drucker sings a chant asking if you are ready to receive. By the time I have listened to that song several times, I am screaming, "YES, I am ready to receive!" especially when I am in my car with the windows rolled up. Remind yourself to receive by posting the question on your bathroom mirror, in the kitchen, car, at your desk—EVERYWHERE!

Are you ready to receive?

Are you ready to receive?

Are you ready to receive?

2. Other reminders to help you practice receiving are:

- Write every day in your journal: I am ready to receive.
- Doodle the words: RECEIVE.
- Sing: "I am ready to receive" to the tune of *Happy Birthday.*
- Dance around singing: "I am ready to receive."
- Shout: "I am ready to receive!"
- Call a friend and say: "I am ready to receive!"
- Repeat often!

3. Meditation is an effective technique for developing your ability to receive. In your quiet time, focus on an affirmation stating you are ready to receive. Sitting with your palms up and open demonstrates your intention to gratefully receive.

4. Make a collage of words that describe the feelings you receive from practicing the art of saying *thank you*—the "aha" moments and self awareness. Add it to your Gold Star *Thank You* Journal or create a memory album.

5. One last *thank you* note idea: Have you ever sent a note saying *thank you* to someone for being able to receive your gift? It happened to me after I accompanied a friend to New York City for her 70th birthday celebration. She wanted to share her joy in giving such a gift to me, as well as thank me for graciously receiving it. She knew what it was like to be on the receiving end of such a gift. Is that the ultimate in giving and receiving? *Thank you*, Marlene!

At the Workplace

As an employee, when you are acknowledged for outstanding work performance, delight in accepting the acknowledgment and appreciation. Welcome it with open arms. You deserve it, you are worthy and you honor the giver. Remember, like the flow of electricity, it is important to keep circulating the energy of saying, *thank you*.

References & Resources

Books

Sharon A. Warren
> *Magnetizing Your Heart's Desire*

Thank You Quotes

> Sarah Ban Breathnach: *Today, declare to the Universe that you are open to receiving all the abundance it's waiting patiently to bestow. Each day offers us the opportunity to learn that as well as giving, it is blessed to receive with grace and a grateful heart.*

> Anthony Robbins: *When you are grateful, fear disappears and abundance appears.*

Afterword. Concluding commentary. Closing statement. A few *last words*.

The *first words* that come to mind are *thank you*. Yes, I
would like to *thank you* for choosing to journey with me
through my philosophy that living the art of saying *thank you*
with thoughts, words and actions creates a most magnificent
way of life. I appreciate the time you have taken and trust
that you feel it has been time well spent.

Next are *words of encouragement* for anyone who
dreams of writing a book. Do it! While I have been blessed
with an abundance of rewarding experiences in my life,
writing THANKYOUOLOGY has definitely been an "E" Ticket
ride. That's Disneyland lingo for thrilling.

With the thrills there can also be some chills. In those
moments where I may have questioned my ability to say the
right words, I am grateful that I never questioned the truths
about which I was writing.

Finally, a few more *poetic words* to say *thank you* for
some of the things I think are the most special in life:

Thank you for all the dreams
Thank you for stardust, angels and moonbeams.

Thank you for unlimited possibilities
Thank you for all capabilities.

Thank you for the tears
Thank you for the cheers.

Thank you for the memories and afterglow
Thank you for life's amazing flow.

Yes, indeed!

What do you mean by the art of saying *thank you*?
I believe there is a science (mechanics) and art (creative) to most everything. The philosophy of THANKYOUOLOGY is about the creative (art) approach to saying *thank you*.

How many *thank you* ideas are in the book? 107

How often does *thank you* appear in the book? 1,047

Why are the words *thank you* italicized?
Each time I changed the font to italics, it gave me the opportunity to think about *thank you*.

Are *thank you* notes *that* important?
Yes! I am willing to bet that advice columnists would agree that not receiving *thank you* notes is one of the most common complaints.

Why is the word "but" nonexistent in the book?
Because there are no "buts" about the philosophy of THANKYOUOLOGY.

Are you a *thank you* coach?
Yes! I coach people in the use of THANKYOUOLOGY principles for personal development, a career change and manifestation of dreams. As a corporate consultant, or what I would call a Chief Morale Officer (CMO), I develop employee recognition programs.

Do you assist with a special *thank you*?
Yes! For individuals or business, I coordinate everything from *thank you* events to custom *thank you* gifts, and even personalized poetic *thank you* notes.

How to contact?   Email: cheryl@THANKYOUOLOGY.com
www.THANKYOUOLOGY.com
www.StarHeart.com

Guidelines for Use:

In the morning…

1. Start with quiet time and deep breathing

2. Date the journal entry.

3. Write at least five *thank you* statements.

4. Create *thank you* affirmations to state your intentions for the day.

In the evening…

Return to your journal before bedtime and give out the gold stars! Acknowledge every step of success. Recognize what showed up as a result of your *thank you* affirmations. Pay attention to the synchronicity that you just can't explain.

....*Day 1*

Date: _June 4, 2012_

Before my day begins, I say *thank you* for:

- Thank-you for time alone.
- Thank you June for coming with.
- Thank You for La Salle Manor.
- Thank you for the beautiful grounds
- Thank you for Devotions & Scriptures

My *thank you* affirmations for today are:

- Thank you for quite time w/ God
- Thank You for study + reading Bible
- Thank you for time of prayer.
- Thank-You enjoying nature
- Thank you Carole for dinner

At the end of my day, I give a gold star for:

- ★ comuning with God
- ★ Being still + knowing God is in charge
- ★ Fellowship w/ Randy & Carol
- ★ a beautiful summer day
- ★ _____

.... *Day 2*

Date: _June 5, 2012_

Before my day begins, I say *thank you* **for:**

Thank you Able to take a early morning walk

Thank you Prayer time w/ Jaime. Thank-you

- Breakfast outside Thank-You
- Walk around Lake
- Reflecting on our day on drive home.

My *thank you* **affirmations for today are:**

THANK Enjoy Nature

You! • Study God word
- Read Proverbs chapters 9·10·11
- Pray and Commune w/ God
- Time for Thank-yous

At the end of my day, I give a gold star for:

★ Our Prayer time together
★ Our walk around the lake
★ Our breakfast outside in the yard
★ Walking the labyrinth
★ Remembering the two days.

....*Day 3*

Date: *June 6 2012*

Before my day begins, I say *thank you* for:

- *Thank You for this day*
- *Thank you for birds that sing*
- *Thank You I can have my nails done*
- *Thank You for Greatgrand babies*
- *Thank you for time w/ Tami*

My *thank you* affirmations for today are:

- *Morning devotions + prayer*
- *Enjoying the sunshine*
- *Time and money to shop*
- *Finding the right walking shoes*
- *Quite Drive in countryside*

At the end of my day, I give a gold star for:

★ *time spent w/ Sophia + Blake*
★ *time w/ Tami, Jeff, Spencer*
★ *Just a good day*
★ *Getting the last pr. of walking shoes*
★

.... Day 4

Date: *June 7-2012*

Before my day begins, I say *thank you* for:

- *Starting it again w/ devotions + prayer*
- *Getting Bea and going to bridge*
- *Thank-you for my bridge ladies*
- *Thank-you for a warm sunny day*
- *Thank-You I can drive*

My *thank you* affirmations for today are:

- *Thank-you I free to go anywhere.*
- *Thank-You for friends*
- *Thank-you for thank-you Cards*
- *Thank-You for eyes to see ears to hear.*
- *Thank-you that my legs + feet are good.*

At the end of my day, I give a gold star for:

★ *Friends that call and just drop by.*
★ *Feel good and busy.*
★ *The night and reading*
★
★

.... Day 5

Date: June 8 2012

Before my day begins, I say *thank you* **for:**

- Thank-You for Another day.
- Thank-You another warm Summer mornin
- Thank you I'm able to clean at church
- Thank you Hands and arms that work
- Thank you for good health

My *thank you* **affirmations for today are:**

- Thank you I will work well w/ other ladies.
- Do my tasks willingly!
- Thank you I'm able to color my hair!
- Thank-You doing my chores w/ ease
- Thank-You I still get Quite time

At the end of my day, I give a gold star for:

- ★ Was able to feed a child for a mo. 40^{00}
- ★ Reading for couple hrs.
- ★ _____
- ★ _____
- ★ _____

....Day 6

Date: June 9 2012

Before my day begins, I say *thank you* for:

- Thanks for The nights Rest
- Thank You a new day
- Thank-You summer's warmth
- Thank you health
- Thank You for independence

My *thank you* affirmations for today are:

- P.E.O. Brunch
- P.E.O Sisterhood
- Thank-You for families to do things with
- Thank-You people to visit with
- Thank-You for what today will bring

At the end of my day, I give a gold star for:

- ★ All my friends in P.E.O.
- ★ Things that happened unplanned
- ★ Fellowship with family members.
- ★ Thanks for a full day of fun.
- ★

.... *Day 7*

Date: June 10 2012

Before my day begins, I say *thank you* for:

- Thank You for Sundays
- Thank You we can worship God
- Thank You Jesus for saving My soul.
- Thank You for a church family.
- Thank you for my personality

My *thank you* affirmations for today are:

- Going to Church
- Making plans for the week.
- Looking forward to a new week.
- Smiles from friends.
-

At the end of my day, I give a gold star for:

★ Just a nice, pleasant
★ Day all day.
★ Good conversation, fellowship,
★ and sharing of thoughts
★ Thank for life.

.... *Day 8*

Date: _June 11_

Before my day begins, I say *thank you* for:

- Thank you for a good nites rest
- Thank you for this new day
- Thank you a busy day
- Still time for devotions
- Bible reading & prayer

My *thank you* affirmations for today are:

- Cutting up fruit at Lois'
- That it is another full day
- Go to Jamie's at 1:0'Clock
- Time with Sophia & Blake.
- The drive in the country.

At the end of my day, I give a gold star for:

★ Quite time
★ Time spent with family
★
★
★

....*Day 9*

Date: June 12 2012

Before my day begins, I say *thank you* for:

- Thank you I have a busy day
- Thank you for starting my day 6:30AM)
- Thank you for my strong body.
- Thank you for a beautiful morning
- Thank you for My faith.

My *thank you* affirmations for today are:

THANK
YOU)

- for helping me to think clear.
- for helping me to work w/ others
- for helping me to not talk about others
- for Lois taking Me to Prisco's
- for getting car serviced + washed needed to get done!

At the end of my day, I give a gold star for:

★ Getting 3 major things done.
★ Laughing with Tami.
★ another pleasant day.
★ Sending a thank you card.
★ Learning a new Bible verse.

He who guards his lips
guards his life
but He who speaks rashly
will come to ruin.

....Day 10

Date: June 13, 2012

Before my day begins, I say *thank you* for:

- Thank you Lord
- Thank you New Day
- Thank you Rested body
- Thank You 1st cup Coffee
- Thank you everything that comes today.

My *thank you* affirmations for today are:

THANK
YOU

- Bridge at my house
- Good cards
- Good Friendships
- Good times
- Good Fun

At the end of my day, I give a gold star for:

★ Cards one hand 6 spades + bid + made it
★ another couple bid + made
★ Its all about Bridge today.
★ The 75° weather today Beautiful
★

....*Day 11*

Date: June 14 2012

Before my day begins, I say *thank you* for:

- Thank you for My Life
- Thank you for so many Blessings
- Thank You for a nice place to live.
- Thank you food so plentiful
- Thank you another busy day.

My *thank you* affirmations for today are:

- Enjoy Grand Circle Breakfast
- Enjoy anything else that comes up
- Enjoy the day
- Call Sarah Happy Birthday
- Call Jeff Happy Birthday

At the end of my day, I give a gold star for:

- ★ Call Sarah + Jeff with B.D Greetings
- ★ Going the Emerson Pottery
- ★ Showing it to Betty + Chuck
- ★ It is so nice Luv it.
- ★ Faye's B.P with friends

....*Day 12*

Date: June 15 2012

Before my day begins, I say *thank you* for:

- Thank you for good nites sleep.
- Thank you new day
- Thank you for feeling good
- Thank You Many things to look forward too.
- Thank You Thank you

My *thank you* affirmations for today are:

THANK

YOU

- Spending 1 hr with Aly + Aaron
- Seeing her engagement ring (Beautiful)
- One on One conversation.
- Thank you for closer dear friends
- Thank you for the Happy feelings.

At the end of my day, I give a gold star for:

- ★ Time w/ grandchildren
- ★ Time w/ dear friend
- ★ Time shared w/ people
- ★ Time for self
- ★ Time for rest

.... *Day 13*

Date: _June 16, 2012_

Before my day begins, I say *thank you* **for:**

- _Thank you ears that hear_
- _Thank you eyes to see_
- _Thank-you nose to smell_
- _Thank you for feeling + touching_
- _Thank-you Healthy body_

My *thank you* **affirmations for today are:**

- _Making Card w Katty_
-
-
-
-

At the end of my day, I give a gold star for:

- ★ _Made Cards from 10 to 8: PM_
- ★ _Made Six different Renies_
- ★ _Six each._
- ★ _Made 36_
- ★ _Oh what fun._

....Day 14

Date: *June 17 2012*

Before my day begins, I say *thank you* for:

- *Thank You for Sundays*
- *Thank you for My Church*
- *Thank you for church families.*
- *Thank you for good rest*
- *Thank you Heavenly Father*

My *thank you* affirmations for today are:

- *Being true to Myself*
- *Speaking truthly*
- *"He who guards his lips*
- *guards his life" (Proverbs 13-3)*
-

At the end of my day, I give a gold star for:

★ *Guarding my lips.*
★ *Just a good day*
★
★
★

....*Day 15*

Date: *June 18 - 2012*

Before my day begins, I say *thank you* **for:**

- *Thank-you for My hands*
- *Thank you for My arms*
- *Thank-you for My Legs*
- *Thank you for feet*
- *Thank-you for Health*

My *thank you* **affirmations for today are:**

- *Driving carefully to Antioch*
- *Fellowship w/ friends*
- _____
- _____
- _____

At the end of my day, I give a gold star for:

★_____

★_____

★_____

★_____

★_____

....Day 16

Date: *June, 19 2012*

Before my day begins, I say *thank you* for:

- *Thank-You friends*
- *Thank you for friends to visit.*
- *Thank-you, friends old & new.*
- *Thank you for friends I enjoy.*
- *Thank-You good fellowship.*

My *thank you* affirmations for today are:

- *meeting for lunch*
- *the new scenery Antioch IL*
- *cards with friends*
- *Staying cool 95°*
-

At the end of my day, I give a gold star for:

★ *Being with Lois.*
★ *Sue*
★ *Barb*
★ *Pleasant day*
★

....*Day 17*

Date: _July 20, 2012_

Before my day begins, I say *thank you* for:

- Thank-you for a new day
- Thank-You good nite rest,
- Thank-You morning coffee
- Thank-You just Thanks

- _____

My *thank you* affirmations for today are:

- The drive home
- The beauty of the drive
- The safe trip home.
- The country side

- _____

At the end of my day, I give a gold star for:

★ Getting back to Batavia
★ Stopping for coffe Caribou
★ with Lois to end
★ our 3 day antioch
★ stay with Suz

....*Day 18*

Date: _July 21 2012._

Before my day begins, I say *thank you* for:

- _Thank-you for my today devotions._
- _Thank-you for eyes to see,_
- _Thank you for Faith, Hope + Love._
- _Thank you for power of prayer_
- _Thank you my Faith._

My *thank you* affirmations for today are:

- _Going to Jami's to price garage sale_
- _The drive out in the country._
- _Seeing the Corn + bean grow._
- _Quite drive_
- _____

At the end of my day, I give a gold star for:

- ★ _Being with with a daughter._
- ★ _Jami Thanking me for the help._
- ★ _____
- ★ _____
- ★ _____

....*Day 19*

Date: June 22 2012

Before my day begins, I say *thank you* for:

- Thank-you for bible reading
- Thank-You for its clear teachings
- Thank you for time to read it, bible
- Thank-You for hearing + answered
- Thank-You Savior Lord God   Prayer

My *thank you* affirmations for today are:

- Helping Rami set up sale
- Going with Sarah to celebrate B's.
- Safety for the day.
- Enjoy the day + night.
- Peace

At the end of my day, I give a gold star for:

- ★ Fellowship family members
- ★ Joy of Grate Granchildren
- ★ Completely bone tired
- ★ Sleep Oh ya!
- ★

.... *Day 20*

Date: June 23 2012

Before my day begins, I say *thank you* for:

- Thank-You for Blessed assurance.
- Thank-you for Blessings.
- Thank-You Blessings unseen.
- Thank-You Jesus.
- Thank-you for my faith.

My *thank you* affirmations for today are:

- a Day of Rest
- Meditation
- Quiet
- To Reflect
- small tasks

At the end of my day, I give a gold star for:

- ★ 7 o'clock till 2:oclock
- ★ Rest & Reading.
- ★
- ★
- ★

..Day 21

Date: *June 25 2012*

Before my day begins, I say *thank you* for:

- *Thank-you 78° weather*
- *Thank-You a busy work day.*
- *Thank-you for the ability.*
- *Thank you for healthy body.*
- *Thank you for a house to work in.*

My *thank you* affirmations for today are:

- *Get 3 things done.*
- *Washing*
- *Ironing*
- *Closet ready for when Bev gets here.*
- *time to read.*

At the end of my day, I give a gold star for:

★ *Stayed home all day.*
★ *Finished 3 big projects*
★ *Good Good Good*
★ *time to read —*
★

....*Day 22*

Date: _June 26-2012_

Before my day begins, I say *thank you* for:

- _Thank you for another comfortable day._
- _Thank you for my legs._
- _Thank you for my feet._
- _Thank-you for healthy bones._
- _Thank-you for abilities to function._

My *thank you* affirmations for today are:

- _Get food ready for tonight_
- _work on Patio sweep & water plant._
- _Clean fridge_
- _____
- _____

At the end of my day, I give a gold star for:

★ _Everything finished_
★ _time to finish Book start another._
★ _____
★ _____
★ _____

....*Day 23*

Date: June 27 2012

Before my day begins, I say *thank you* for:

- Thank-you for my voice
- Thank-you for My Mouth
- Thank-You for reasoning Power.
- Thank-you for good life.
- Thank-You for Me.

My *thank you* affirmations for today are:

- Talking with friends
- Lunching with good friends.
- Good devotions + prayer time.
- praying for Dear Friend Sue.
- God keep her in your loving arms,

At the end of my day, I give a gold star for:

- ★ _____
- ★ Lunch + time spent with friends
- ★ _____
- ★ _____
- ★ _____

....*Day 24*

Date: *June 28 2012*

Before my day begins, I say *thank you* for:

- *Thank-you for cool morning.*
- *Thank you for the sunshine,*
- *Thank-you for flowers*
- *Thank-you for birds that sing*
- *Thank you God for everything.*

My *thank you* affirmations for today are:

- *Coffee with Cottage girls.*
- *Gert, June, Janet dear friends.*
- *Getting ready for trip to Lincoln Ic.*
- *Keeping cool*
- *Keeping My Cool!*

At the end of my day, I give a gold star for:

★_____

★_____

★_____

★_____

★_____

....*Day 25*

Date: June 29 - 2012

Before my day begins, I say *thank you* for:

- Thank you for time
- Thank you for time to pray.
- Thank You for time to play
- Thank-you for time to read
- Thank-you for today.

My *thank you* affirmations for today are:

- Dayly duties
- paper work
- Pick up put away
-
-

At the end of my day, I give a gold star for:

- ★ Finished the day in good shape
- ★ Not to much happened
- ★ Long talk with Joyce got home from Trip!
- ★
- ★

.... *Day 26*

Date: _June 30_ 2012

Before my day begins, I say *thank you* for:

- Thank you for 1 busy month.
- Thank you for warm hot days.
- Thank you for rain last nite.
- Thank you for fun things to do.
- Thank you for good nite rest.

My *thank you* affirmations for today are:

- Get some things ready for Bro.
- Go to graduation party (abby)
- a slow day
- _____
- _____

At the end of my day, I give a gold star for:

- ★ _____
- ★ Abbys Grad party was
- ★ fun saw old friends &
- ★ new people
- ★ _____

.... *Day 27*

Date: _July 1-2012_

Before my day begins, I say *thank you* for:

- _Thank-you for church family_
- _Thank-You for Sunday to reflect on_
- _the new wk ahead._
- _Thank-you your earth + its beauty._
- _Thank You for your word (Bible)_

My *thank you* affirmations for today are:

- _attending church_
- _time w Dawn + Scat._
- _Did not go to Scots Bad storm_
- _____
- _____

At the end of my day, I give a gold star for:

★ _Needed + got rain_
★ _It poured_
★ _Electric out for 4 hrs._
★ _____
★ _____

....*Day 28*

Date: _July 2 -2012_

Before my day begins, I say *thank you* for:

- Thank you for This new wk.
- Thank you for things to do.
- Thank-you for health
- Thank you for beauty of nature.
- Thank you God for life.

My *thank you* affirmations for today are:

- Getting ready to leave for Lincoln
- Getting house hold duties done
- _____
- _____
- _____

At the end of my day, I give a gold star for:

★ Ready to go to Lincoln Il
★ Ready for Bev's visit
★ _____
★ _____
★ _____

....*Day 29*

Date: _July 3-2012_

Before my day begins, I say *thank you* for:

- Thank-you good nite rest
- Thank-You rested enough
- to leave for Lincoln
- at 6 o'clock, hah!
- Thank-You for the plan.

My *thank you* affirmations for today are:

- Got in Lincoln at 9:15
- Shelley talked me to her home.
- Good trip.
- not bad drive
-

At the end of my day, I give a gold star for:

★ Got there safely.
★ Enjoy the company at Shelley's
★ Planned our trip for tomorrow.
★
★

....Day 30

Date: July 4 · 2012

Before my day begins, I say *thank you* for:

- Thank you for friends homes
- Thank you beautiful surroundings
- Thank you for the farm land
- Thank You for gardens
- Thank You for places to see.

My *thank you* affirmations for today are:

- Lincolns house
- Old Springfield capital
- movies & talks about Pres Lincoln
- to learn as much as I can
- guides to show us around

At the end of my day, I give a gold star for:

- ★ Lincoln home
- ★ Old Springfield Capital.
- ★ All the history of Springfield.
- ★ Seeing it with Bev, Shelley + Phil.
- ★ a great day

July

Thank you for thank you ology Book

Thank you for what Ive learned

...................Thank You Rhymes

Angels

Animals

Children/Babies

Entertainment

Finances/Wealth/Prosperity

Food

Health/Physical

Miscellaneous

Nature

Relationaships/People/Friends

Things

Angels

Thank you for the help of angels from above
Thank you for all of your light and love.

Animals

Thank you for crackers and a cup of soup
Thank you for birds that even go poop.

———

Thank you for the birds and bees
Thank you for my sturdy knees.

———

Thank you for healthy fingernails
Thank you for cats and puppy dog tails.

———

Thank you for winter and spring
Thank you for the birds that sing.

———

Thank you for ideas that keep coming through
Thank you also for trips to the zoo.

———

Thank you for people who follow through on their word
Thank you for African animals that travel in a herd.

———

Thank you for arms that give lots of hugs
Thank you for even those cute little bugs.

———

Thank you for the ocean and fishes in the sea
Thank you for the tiniest, little green pea.

———

Thank you for friends that stop by unannounced
Thank you for kitty cats and doggies that pounce.

———

Thank you for socks that keep my feet warm
Thank you for bees that hide when they swarm.

———

Thank you for greeting cards that come via e-mail
Thank you for those elongated fish story tales.

———

Thank you for butterflies that spread their wings
Thank you for breezy days and sitting in swings.

Children/Babies

Thank you for a baby's cry
Thank you for questions that start with "Why."

———

Thank you kids who follow the rules
Thank you for dedicated teachers in schools.

———

Thank you for weddings that unite couples in marriage
Thank you for bassinets and the strolling carriage.

Entertainment

Thank you for rainbows that double in size
Thank you for those parties that definitely surprise.

———

Thank you for designers of humorous cartoons
Thank you for great big colorful balloons.

———

Thank you for the magic of Disneyland
Thank you for the fingers on my hand.

———————

Thank you for the jokes and things that make us giggle
Thank you for jello and how it jiggles.

———————

Thank you for all that there is
Thank you for people in show biz.

———————

Thank you for the month of June
Thank you for melodic tunes.

———————

Thank you for Disney characters like Mickey Mouse
Thank you for my wonderful house.

———————

Thank you for movies that make me laugh
Thank you for my better half.

———————

Thank you for bright colored ribbons and bows
Thank you for the dazzle of entertaining shows!

———————

Thank you for people who teach me new things
Thank you for those who really know how to sing.

———————

Thank you for the circus and those skillful acts
Thank you for hammers, nails and tiny tacks!

———————

Thank you for magicians who pull things out of a hat
Thank you for comedians who joke about this and that.

———

Thank you for the letter "R"
Thank you for a day of golf "under par."

———

Thank you for Hollywood's night of Academy Awards
Thank you for basketball hoops and those fast skateboards.

———

Thank you for good news on TV and in the papers
Thank you for fun and safe little capers.

———

Thank you for people from all walks of life
Thank you for classic characters like Barney Fife.

Finances/Wealth/Prosperity

Thank you for radiant health
Thank you for prosperity and wealth.

———

Thank you for showing me how to let go
Thank you for the law of reaping what I sow.

———

Thank you for diamonds and gold
Thank you for times when I need to be bold.

———

Thank you for the day I got my own phone
Thank you for qualifying for my first home loan.

———

Thank you for money to spend
Thank you for I know it never ends.

————

Thank you for pennies, nickels and dimes
Thank you for those clocks with neat little chimes.

Food

Thank you for water that ripples on the lake
Thank you for the times I get to bake.

————

Thank you for food that tastes so good
Thank you for being understood.

————

Thank you for delicious food to eat
Thank you for those special treats.

————

Thank you for paper and pens
Thank you for eggs laid by hens.

————

Thank you for the time to relax
Thank you for grocery-filled sacks.

————

Thank you for sushi and California rolls
Thank you for those green hills and knolls.

————

Thank you for bread making machines
Thank you for black, red and pinto beans.

————

Health/Physical

Thank you for helping me get things done
Thank you for my legs that enable me to run.

———

Thank you for healthy fingernails
Thank you for cats and puppy dog tails.

———

Thank you for my eyes that see
Thank you for taking care of me.

———

Thank you for the ability to walk
Thank you for being able to talk.

———

Thank you for my eyes and ears
Thank you for those happy tears.

———

Thank you for my heart open wide
Thank you for my funny side.

———

Thank you for the thrill of a surprise
Thank you for beautiful, sparkling eyes.

———

Thank you for holding my hand
Thank you for every particle of sand.

———

Thank you for the month of December
Thank you for the ability to remember.

———

Thank you for my smiling face
Thank you for the human race.

————

Thank you for help when I need it quick
Thank you for hair that looks really slick.

Miscellaneous

Thank you for the sound of "hush"
Thank you for when I don't have to rush.

————

Thank you for those who understand computers
Thank you for those ancient things made of pewter.

————

Thank you for being so blessed
Thank you for the words, YES, YES, YES!

————

Thank you for things that go around
Thank you for all of those unusual sounds.

————

Thank you for those who recognize my gifts
Thank you for vitamins that give me a lift.

————

Thank you for making all my dreams come true
Thank you for the saying, "Who knew?"

————

Thank you for the delight of a simple pleasure
Thank you for tools that help us measure.

————

Thank you for those times for tears
Thank you for the reflections of mirrors.

————

Thank you for the inventor of rope
Thank you for the wonderful feeling of hope.

————

Thank you for designers of humorous cartoons
Thank you for great big colorful balloons.

————

Thank you for click art that makes me an artist
Thank you for short reviews that give me "the gist."

————

Thank you for baubles and bangles galore
Thank you for lectures that aren't a bore.

————

Thank you for energy and power
Thank you for every hour.

————

Thank you for gifts that I receive
Thank You for the thoughts I believe.

————

Thank you for feeling so good inside
Thank you for our country pride.

————

Thank you for the candle's light
Thank you for my sleep at night.

————

Thank you for all I have to give
Thank you for the precious life I live.

———

Thank you for thoughtful words to say
Thank you for everything this day.

———

Thank you for making clear my way
Thank you for this I pray.

———

Thank you for my actions so kind
Thank you for the intelligence of my mind.

———

Thank you for showing me how
Thank you for being in "the now."

———

Thank you for the greatness of spirit
Thank you for speaking so I can "hear it."

———

Thank you for the color green
Thank you for helping me say what I mean.

———

Thank you for tears that flow
Thank you for the truth I know.

———

Thank you for beauty and grace
Thank you for things made of lace.

———

Thank you for feeling safe and secure
Thank you for all things pure.

———————

Thank you for raindrops that fall
Thank you for time to go to the mall.

———————

Thank you for smiles so bright
Thank you for all my might.

———————

Thank you for my job at work
Thank you for duties I don't shirk.

———————

Thank you for poems that rhyme
Thank you for precious time.

———————

Thank you for the color red
Thank you for guys named Ted.

———————

Thank you for things that amaze me
Thank you for things that don't faze me.

———————

Thank you for words that truly express
Thank you for gratitude and happiness.

———————

Thank you for ideas that inspire
Thank you for those feelings of desire.

———————

Thank you for words that come out funny
Thank you for when he calls me "honey."

———

Thank you for those moments of pure romance
Thank you for every circumstance.

———

Thank you for all I have to give and receive
Thank you for being bothered less by a "pet peeve."

———

Thank you for words like perseverance
Thank you for automatic deterrents.

———

Thank you for gifts both big and small
Thank you for feeling ever so tall.

Nature

Thank you for sushi and California rolls
Thank you for those green hills and knolls.

———

Thank you for trees and their bark
Thank you for guiding me out of the dark.

———

Thank you for my cup that runneth over
Thank you for those little four leaf clovers.

———

Thank you for those cute little leprechauns
Thank you for the glory of morning dawns.

———

Thank you for rainbows that dance across the sky
Thank you for phrases like "oh me, oh my."

————

Thank you for tulips that pop up in the spring
Thank you for the telephone when it rings.

————

Thank you for the red rose and what it means
Thank you for how the Tower of Pisa leans.

————

Thank you for galaxies that are endless it's true
Thank you for candles that shine brightly for two.

————

Thank you for unexpected surprises
Thank you for those incredible morning sunrises.

————

Thank you for the clouds so white
Thank you for the magic of the night.

————

Thank you for winter and spring
Thank you for the birds that sing.

————

Thank you for laughter and fun
Thank you for the early morning sun.

————

Thank you for the moon and stars
Thank you for things that come in jars.

————

Thank you for the flowers' scented smell
Thank you for keeping me well.

————

Thank you for holidays
Thank you for trees that sway.

————

Thank you for roses that bloom
Thank you for my very own room.

————

Thank you for the day I was born
Thank you for roses and even their thorns.

————

Thank you for gentleness in the breeze
Thank you for the trees and all their leaves.

————

Thank you for rainbows and fluffy white snow
Thank you for experiences that help me grow.

————

Thank you for holding my hand
Thank you for every particle of sand.

————

Thank you for the longer days
Thank you for sunshine breaking through the haze.

Relationships/People/Friends

Thank you for people who teach me new things
Thank you for those who really know how to sing.

————

Thank you for universal truth
Thank you for loving youth.

————

Thank you for my friends and family
Thank you for peace and serenity.

————

Thank you for my life
Thank you for the joy of being a wife.

————

Thank you for my special mate
Thank you for everything to date.

————

Thank you for surprises filled with joy
Thank you for little girls and boys.

————

Thank you for my in-laws
Thank you for my time to pause.

————

Thank you for people that lend a hand
Thank you for feeling that all is grand.

————

Thank you for my nephew and niece
Thank you for the protection of the police.

————

Thank you for my sister who's my friend as well
Thank you for those people who treat me swell.

————

187

Thank you for colors that add such beauty
Thank you for people that honor their duty.

———

Thank you for people who follow through on their word
Thank you for African animals that travel in a herd.

———

Thank you for the family tree
Thank you for the branch just for me.

———

Thank you for friends that keep in touch
Thank you for words like many and much.

———

Thank you for neighbors who are friendly and kind
Thank you for time to relax and unwind.

———

Thank you for galaxies that are endless it's true
Thank you for candles that shine brightly for two.

Things

Thank you for the roof over my head
Thank you for my cozy bed.

———

Thank you for chairs that make me sit up straight
Thank you for alarm clocks that get me awake.

———

Thank you for tulips that pop up in the spring
Thank you for the telephone when it rings.

———

Thank you for my beautiful car
Thank you for the way things are.

————

Thank you for warm clothes to wear
Thank you for the ability to share.

————

Thank you for something I just bought
Thank you for giving it "all I've got!"

————

Thank you for the automobile
Thank you for the invention of the wheel.

————

Thank you for swimming pools that let me splash
Thank you for when I won the hundred yard dash.

————

Thank you for clocks that go tick tock
Thank you for finding that missing sock.

......................*Your Thank You Rhymes*

........................*Your Thank You Rhymes*

..........................*Your Thank You Rhymes*